Jenny Morris is a disabled woman, feminist and freelance writer/researcher. She is the author of *Pride Against Prejudice: Transforming Attitudes to Disability* (The Women's Press, 1991), and has edited *Able Lives: Women's Experience of Paralysis* (The Women's Press, 1989) and *Alone Together: Voices of Single Mothers* (The Women's Press, 1992). She is also the author of *Independent Lives? Community Care and Disabled People.*

D0797134

Also by Jenny Morris from The Women's Press:

Able Lives: Women's Experience of Paralysis ed (1989)
Pride Against Prejudice: Transforming Attitudes to Disability (1991)
Alone Together: Voices of Single Mothers ed (1992)

Other titles of interest from The Women's Press:

Mustn't Grumble: Writing by Disabled Women (1994)
ed Lois Keith
Past Due: A Story of Disability, Pregnancy and Birth (1991)
Anne Finger

Encounters
with
Strangers

Feminism *and* Disability

JENNY MORRIS, EDITOR

First published by The Women's Press Ltd, 1996
A member of the Namara Group
34 Great Sutton Street, London EC1V 0DX

Collection copyright © Jenny Morris 1996

British Library Cataloguing-in-Publication Data
A catalogue record for this book is available from the British
Library

ISBN 0 7043 4400 9

Typeset in Palatino by Contour Typesetters, Southall, London
Printed and bound in Great Britain by
BPC Paperbacks Ltd
A member of
The British Printing Company Ltd

CONTENTS

ACKNOWLEDGEMENTS

This book has its origins in a number of meetings held amongst disabled women in 1993 and 1994. We discussed our experiences of the disabled people's and the women's movements and many women felt that they wanted to explore further a number of issues of concern to them. We talked also about the links which need to be made between women with physical/sensory impairments, women with learning difficulties and women who are mental health system survivors. These discussions were a crucial part of the development of this book and I am very grateful to all who took part.

Experiences of disability and impairment – together with other pressures of daily life – meant that a number of women who would have liked to contribute to this book were not, in the event, able to do so. Nevertheless, the discussions which we had and the work which they did were very important and will no doubt be part of the continuing development of the themes raised in the book.

While my aim as editor has been to bring together key interventions in the fields of feminism and disability, I am well aware of the debt that we owe to those who went before us – particularly to disabled women who do not have the opportunity to get their thinking published. This book does not attempt a definitive account of feminism and disability. There are many themes which need further development – in particular the links between the different parts of the disabled people's movement referred to above.

Finally, my thanks to the contributors for their hard work and their patience. It has taken a long time to get this book together but I think they can be justifiably proud of themselves for sticking with it.

Jenny Morris

INTRODUCTION
Jenny Morris

This book has its origins in two ongoing conversations: one with feminism, the other with the disabled people's movement. Disability is a women's issue – in that the majority of disabled people are women – yet the experience of disabled women has been largely absent from feminism's concerns and, within the disabled people's movement, has tended to be tacked on as a 'special interest'.

In this opening chapter, which will also serve to introduce the reader to the chapters which follow, I want to explore these two dialogues and challenge both feminism and the disabled people's movement to recognise the importance of disabled women's experiences.

In the past, both non-disabled feminists and the men who dominate the disabled people's movement have been strangers to the concerns of disabled women. Our encounters with both groups have often made us feel powerless for we have either been treated as invisible or our experiences have been defined for us. This book invites these strangers to enter our world, on our terms, and to commence a dialogue on the basis of respect and equality.

Disabled women and feminism

Amongst all the books I have on my shelves about feminist knowledge, philosophy and politics, research which deals with areas of women's lives such as employment and motherhood, writings on domestic violence, reproductive rights, feminist perspectives on the welfare state, on child abuse and so on – not one deals with the experiences of disabled women. The little analysis that there is of our lives appears as a 'special' area of study, in (a very few) separate books and articles, and is often couched in terms of asking whether and how women with physical or sensory impairments and/or learning diffi- culties, encounter a 'double disadvantage' because of their experience of sexism and disability. Usually these 'special' studies attempt to assess which is 'worse', which has the most serious effect on a woman's life chances.

I always feel uncomfortable reading about our lives and concerns when they are presented in these terms. When Susan Lonsdale writes, 'For women, the status of "disabled" compounds their status of being "female" to create a unique type of oppression' (Lonsdale, 1990, p. 82), I feel burdened by disadvantage. When Margaret Lloyd states that the issue for disabled women is 'the dilemma of identity for an individual experiencing multiple disadvantage and oppression' (Lloyd, 1992, p. 208), I feel a victim.

Perhaps I should feel grateful for these attempts to make visible the experiences of women like me, since in other feminist analyses of women's lives, disabled women have been conspicuous by their absence. So maybe I'm being unfair: all I know is that such writings do not empower me.

We have to find a way of making our experiences visible, sharing them with each other and with non-disabled people, in a way that – while drawing attention to the difficulties in our lives – does not undermine our wish to assert our self-worth. In fact, feminist writing does not usually victimise the (non-disabled) women whose lives are the subject of research and analysis. Feminist analyses of women's oppression are them- selves a way of asserting resistance, of struggling against oppression. Studies of women's experiences – although they are studies of the difficulties that women face in their lives – rarely present them as passive victims.

A representation of our lives which combines a feminist and a disability rights perspective will be rooted in the resistance to oppression; it will itself be part of the struggle against the discrimination and prejudice which disabled women ex- perience and, as such, will focus not just on our exclusion but also on our survival. In this book Sally French's account of girls with visual impairment who were excluded from mainstream education, sent away from their families to a residential 'special' school, is an account of disadvantage and discrimination (Chapter One). Yet it is also an account of survival. 'Long-term incarceration' she writes, 'can have profound and lasting effects on those subjected to it. It is a tribute to the women [interviewed] that they emerged from this experience capable and warm human beings'.

As far as the question of whether it is 'gender or disability', or indeed 'race or sexuality' which are the more important determinants of experience, I don't find this way of looking at our lives very helpful either. I think this is partly because our experiences are not fragmented into analytical categories. When Ayesha Vernon (Chapter Two) interviewed other Black and ethnic minority women, she found that 'Disabled Black and ethnic minority women experience a multiplicity of barriers resulting from the combination of disablism, racism and sexism.' While some of the women felt that at certain times and certain places it was race, disability or gender which determined their experiences, as one of them put it, 'it happens singularly, plurally and multiply, and it's the totality that counts at the end of the day. You are completely thought of as inferior because you are all three things.

Before I acquired a physical impairment, it was sexism which dominated my interaction with the public and private world: now it is other people's reaction to me as a *disabled* woman which structures my experience. It is also my impairment which prevents most non-disabled women from identifying their interests with mine. An incident which was part of my disabling experience in a workplace neatly illustrates this.

When a male work colleague threatened me because I parked in such a way that my car blocked his car in – I was forced to do this because a non-disabled person had parked in the space reserved for me as a disabled person – there was a limit to my female colleagues' sense of outrage. His harassment was of me as a disabled *woman*: he would not have behaved towards a disabled man in quite the same way but, on the other hand, it was his reaction to my impairment which formed a key element of his perception and actions. Thus when one woman challenged him about his behaviour, he confided that he felt 'sorry' for me. This diluted her perception of his threatened violence towards me; she no longer saw him as the threat I did. I was all too aware by then that 'feeling sorry' for a disabled person is part and parcel of hostility, of an inability to identify with him/her and entirely compatible with a tendency to inflict physical and/or verbal abuse. Since, however, this woman's perception of me also contained a 'feeling sorry' element, the man's sharing of his feelings towards me created a commonality between them which undermined her common identity with me as another woman.

Unlike the non-disabled feminists whose focus on the 'double disadvantage' of disability and sexism can only feed into the negative attitudes of those 'feeling sorry' for us, this book focuses on understanding our realities in the context of our struggle, our resistance, our survival. Like the feminists of the 1960s and 1970s who 'discovered' women's exclusion from history, who exposed women's experience of poverty and discrimination, who insisted that violence against women must be recognised and stopped, we are motivated by a sense of outrage and injustice. We are outraged that our voices are silenced so that our oppression is not recognised; we define as injustice the exclusion of disabled people from mainstream society.

In doing this we share with each other, and develop an understanding of, the detailed reality of our daily lives, using such politicisation of the personal to make sense of our experiences of prejudice and discrimination. It is from understanding the kind of encounter I described above that we gain strength, in the same way that feminists of the 1960s and 1970s gained strength from understanding the nature of the daily interaction between men and women, the deep-seated unequal power relationships which we struggle to change. As Lois Keith writes in Chapter Three,

Disabled people have to work continually against destructive forces which see us as powerless, passive and unattractive. It seems that no matter how cheerfully and positively we attempt to go out into the world, we are bound to be confronted by someone whose response to our lack of ordinariness, our difference from the norm leaves us feeling powerless and angry. Trying to understand the complicated feelings which arise out of our everyday encounters with the world is central to the lives of all disabled people.

The relevance of a feminist perspective

Although we feel betrayed and excluded by feminist analysis and activism, many disabled women still feel that key aspects of feminism have great relevance to how we experience oppression and discrimination. Like women generally, many disabled people live in intimate relationships with those who have greater social and economic power than them. Like women, disabled people's politicisation has its roots in the assertion that 'the personal is political', that our personal experiences of being denied opportunities are not to be explained by our bodily limitations (our impairments) but by the social, environmental and attitudinal barriers which are a daily part of our lives.

Feminist investigations highlight the issues that are at the centre of women's lives. As Miriam David writes, 'I take feminist to mean social investigations which do not render women and girls invisible but which seek to highlight social issues from the standpoint of women.' (David, 1991, p. 95) Feminists have therefore researched motherhood, violence, employment, poverty – all the aspects of women's lives that are influenced by the social construction of gender and its economic and personal consequences.

These are all issues of relevance to disabled women – even though our experiences are rarely incorporated into feminist research in these areas. The exclusion of disabled women means that the accounts of women's experiences are incomplete because a whole important group of women are missing from the picture. Moreover, this exclusion also renders feminist theory and analysis incomplete for there is no attempt to understand the interactions between the two social constructs of gender and disability. If research and analysis seeks 'to highlight social issues from the standpoint of *disabled* women' then feminist investigations will take on new ways of looking at women's experiences.

All forms of prejudice have at their heart a refusal to identify with a person's reality, setting them apart from common humanity. This is a very important part of the prejudice experienced by disabled people, based as it often is on an assumption that the quality of our lives is so poor that they are not worth living – and therefore an unwillingness to identify with our reality. Unfortunately, the way that some feminist sociologists have excluded disabled women's subjective reality from their research has colluded with these prejudicial assumptions.

This exclusion has been particularly apparent in the research and analysis carried out over the last 15 years or so on 'community care'. Both Lois Keith and myself have challenged the way that feminist researchers have defined those providing unpaid assistance to disabled and older people as 'carers' and those who receive such assistance as 'dependent people' (Keith, 1994; Morris, 1993). Disabled and older women's voices have been entirely absent from such research and, in spite of our criticisms they remain largely absent from the most recent developments in this area, namely the identification of 'children as carers'. This is the subject of Chapter Four, where Lois Keith and I examine how sociologists and social services professionals are constructing the children of disabled parents as 'young carers' and their parents as 'dependants'. We argue that a failure amongst professionals to focus instead on meeting disabled parents' need for practical assistance colludes with the government's community care policy of relying on the unpaid work which goes on within families. Identifying the children of disabled parents as 'young carers' both undermines the parent's right to assistance (contained within the Chronically Sick and Disabled Persons Act 1970) and fails to protect children's rights as laid down in the Children Act 1989.

It is particularly disappointing that feminists have failed to highlight the way the 'young carers' debate is part of the general attack on single mothers, which has been such an important part of the political landscape of the 1990s. Single, divorced and separated mothers are over-represented amongst those whose children are identified as 'young carers'. As we point out,

> The particular difficulties experienced by single disabled mothers and the way that the debate on 'young carers' has fed into the debate on single parents – both of them containing an implicit if not explicit attack on women's ability to parent without the presence of a man in the household – remain unexplored, but important, issues.

It is clear to us that, if feminist investigations start to include disabled women, then the very terms of the analysis will have to change. Margaret Kennedy makes this point clearly in her discussion and analysis concerning abuse experienced by disabled children (Chapter Five). Starting from the position that 'official definitions of physical and emotional abuse and neglect fail to encompass a full range of abusive experiences that disabled adults speak about', she looks at the evidence of disabled children's experiences, at the barriers to disclosure and action, concluding that 'We need research which is based on the direct experience of disabled adults and children; in particular we need to make it possible for adult survivors to come together to articulate and share their experiences . . .'

One of the most successful 'feminist investigations' of the 1970s and 1980s has been that concerning domestic violence. Research and activism alike have drawn attention to the violence that women experience within their own homes, redefined this violence as unacceptable, challenged the legal system to take it seriously and, through the women's refuge movement, provided opportunities for women to leave violent relationships. Yet none of the studies of domestic violence have considered the issue from the perspective of disabled women and it is therefore hardly surprising that only recently have women's refuges started to look at how they can provide a service to disabled women. As with non-disabled women, disabled women face the issue of naming the violence they experience and getting others to recognise it. Feminist investigations of violence experienced by disabled women within their home would highlight abuse in Homes as well as homes and by perpetrators who are paid carers as well as those who are family members.

Liz Kelly reminds us that 'The *Oxford English Dictionary* defines violence as involving damage to the self. The damage may be physical, emotional, psychological and/or material. Violation can be of the body, of the mind or of trust. The exercise of violence involves the denial of the victims' will and autonomy.' (Kelly, 1988, p. 39). Denial of will and autonomy is a daily feature of many disabled peoples lives; we need feminist research and analysis to put this under the same kind of spotlight that has been brought to non-disabled women's lives.

Whereas services have developed for women experiencing domestic violence (as defined by non-disabled women) and/or rape, there has been very little service development for disabled women experiencing abuse and violence. The Powerhouse – a group of women with learning difficulties and their allies – was formed in response to the experience of abuse and the lack of refuges specifically for women with learning difficulties. In Chapter Six the women involved in the Powerhouse tell of how they came together and how they have developed the first refuge of its kind, the Beverley Lewis House, which caters especially for women with learning difficulties, including those with physical and/or sensory impairments.

If disabled women's concerns form part of future feminist investigations, this cannot fail to influence the political demands which women make. One of the most contentious areas of discussion between feminists and the disability movement has been that concerning abortion. Just as feminist analysis has framed the community care debate in terms that make assumptions about whether disabled people's lives are worth living, so has the 'women's right to choose' debate assumed that a 'handicapped foetus' means a poor quality of life for both child and mother. Ruth Bailey's chapter, Chapter Seven, in looking at the implications of prenatal testing for disabled people in the light of recent advances in genetic knowledge, challenges both the feminist and the disabled people's movement's perspective on these issues. From her wide-ranging review of the debate, she identifies that

> there is considerable scope for oppressive ideas of normality and what it is to be human . . . to inform the political, scientific and medical decision-making processes associated with the new genetic technology. These oppressive ideas have implications for disabled and non-disabled women alike and there is a clear case for the feminist and disabled people's movements to open up a dialogue in order to protect and promote women's interests generally in this context.

The segregation that dominates disabled people's experience of education, and the discrimination that determines our unequal access to the labour market, means that few disabled women are currently in a position to attract funding to carry out research on the issues that really concern us. Nasa Begum's chapter is an illustration of the kind of work that would result if we were able to create the space for feminist investigations of disabled women's experiences. Her research arose out of an issue that is of keen interest to us – our consumption of health services – but which also tends to be obscured by the disabled people's movement's 'resistance to disability being construed as a catalogue of medical problems'. As she points out in Chapter Eight, 'In the past disabled people have fought so hard to challenge the medicalisation of their lives and experiences that concerns about health needs have tended to be minimised.' This leads us to the second theme which runs throughout this book: our dialogue with the disabled people's movement.

Women and the disability movement
While the disabled people's movement has made important gains in recent years for all disabled people, it has tended to treat women's concerns as particular or marginal: women's experiences and interests have not been central to the movement's campaigns.

Disabled women have a particular perspective on one of the

most important campaigns waged by the disabled people's movement, the campaign for 'direct payments' – cash grants that make it possible for those who need personal assistance to purchase the help they need. This campaign came out of the Independent Living Movement, an international movement of disabled people which asserts that physical, sensory and/or intellectual impairment does not *in itself* mean that people cannot exercise choice and control in their lives. The concept of indepedent living insists that biology is not destiny. Impairment does not *necessarily* create dependency and a poor quality of life; rather it is the lack of control over the physical help needed which takes away people's independence. The provision of personal assistance over which disabled people have control is therefore a crucial part of achieving inde-pendent living and, for those that wish it, the ability to purchase personal assistance – through cash grants made available for the purpose – is a key route to such independence.

Pioneers of the Independent Living Moment have played a key role in supporting other disabled people to be confident about becoming employers of personal assistants, about establishing situations where they receive assistance in an empowering, rather than a disempowering, way. Yet the particular needs of disabled women are often unrecognised in that their role as 'care*givers*' remains invisible. For example, the job description for a personal assistant detailed in the publi-cation *Making Our Own Choices* (Barnes, 1994) contains no reference to the possibility of a personal assistant enabling an employer (i.e. the disabled person) to look after children or run a home.

When I looked at the experience of people who need personal assistance in their daily lives (Morris, 1993), it was apparent that, for women, the *giving* of personal assistance and support to others within their household was an important role. Disabled women want personal assistance which enables them to look after children, to run a home, to look after parents or others who need help themselves. In contrast, the disabled people's movement has tended to focus on personal assistance which enables paid employment and other activities outside the home. These things are of course important for disabled women as well but the disabled people's movement has, so far, failed to give enough prominence to the fact that the choice and control which is at the heart of the movement's concept of independent living must also be concerned with the private world of the family and personal relationships. Independent living for both disabled men and women is as much about being able to participate in caring relationships as it is about participating in the public world of work (see Morris, 1995).

Over the last 20 years or so, the disabled people's movement has made considerable advances in persuading the non-disabled world to adopt what we call the 'social model' of disability. This means recognising that people who have physical, sensory or intellectual impairments, or mental/emotional distress, are denied opportunities, discriminated against and excluded by the barriers that society creates. It means focusing, not on our impairments – what is 'wrong' with our bodies or our minds – but on what is wrong with the way society is organised. In other words, focusing on the prejudice that we experience, inaccessible physical and communication environments, the failure to put resources into enabling technology, and other socially created barriers.

Sexism and racism refer to the oppression experienced by women and by Black people; disability refers to the oppression experienced by people with physical, sensory or intellectual impairments, or mental/emotional distress. Julie McNamara puts the argument clearly for all disabled people when she makes the case, in Chapter Nine, that survivors of the mental health system are part of the disabled people's movement.

It is society that disables people. It is the combination of personal and institutionalised prejudices that create disabling environments. People who have been through the mental health systems or have otherwise acquired a psychiatric history often find their access to employment, housing and other necessities to a good quality life barred by others' subtle and not-so-subtle discriminatory behaviour. People with mental distress are disabled. Disability is about removing people's power, or denying access to power.

Those who use the mental health system are disabled by the enormity of societal and personal prejudices directed at us.

It is the social model of disability with its emphasis on social and economic oppression rather than individual inadequacies and personal tragedies which forces a recognition of disability as a civil rights issue. By the time this book is published we will have at least some form of anti-discrimination legislation in Britain – whether it is the limited law proposed by the Conservative government in power at the time of writing or the more comprehensive civil rights bill put forward by the disabled people's movement. The extent of our achievement in changing people's way of thinking is illustrated by the fact that it was only in 1983 that the government threw out a bill which proposed to outlaw discrimination against disabled people by employers, arguing that no such discrimination existed. This argument was possible because the dominant attitude towards disabled people was one of benevolent paternalism, an attitude which allows no room for the recognition of prejudice and discrimination. This had particular relevance for me at the time as my employer – a local education authority whose motto was 'Progress with Humanity' – was trying to sack me following an accident which left me permanently paralysed. It was difficult at that time, such a short time ago really, for people to recognise this action as discrimination. After all, everyone felt so sorry for me – and wasn't it a tragedy that I would never walk, or work (they thought), again?

The social model of disability has not only started to change general social attitudes towards disabled people, it has liberated individual disabled people from the burden of personal tragedy, the oppression of individual inadequacies. It is difficult to overestimate the impact the social model has had on disabled people's lives. As Liz Crow says in Chapter Ten:

Discovering this way of thinking about my experiences was the proverbial raft in stormy areas. It gave me an understanding of my life, shared with thousands, even millions, of other people around the world, and I clung to it.

For years now this social model of disability has enabled

me to confront, survive and even surmount countless situations of exclusion and discrimination. It has been my mainstay, as it has been for the wider disabled people's movement. It has enabled a vision of ourselves free from the constraints of disability and provided a direction for our commitment to social change. It has played a central role in promoting disabled people's individual self-worth, collective identity and political organisation. I don't think it is an exaggeration to say that the social model has saved lives.

Perhaps it is a sign of the developing maturity of the disabled people's movement that we are now at a stage where we can look at a way of thinking which was revolutionary only 20 years ago, and say, hang on a minute, this isn't quite right. When we were thinking about getting this book off the ground, we organised a series of meetings of disabled women. Liz Crow had already published an earlier version of the chapter which appears in this book in *Coalition*, one of the journals of the disabled people's movement, and our first discussions addressed some of the problems she raises about the social model.

Generally, there was a concern amongst some disabled women that the way our experience was being politicised didn't leave much room for acknowledging our experience of our bodies; that too often there wasn't room for talking about the experience of impairment, that a lot of us feel pressured into just focusing on disability, just focusing on social barriers. For many this feels a very dangerous thing to say, in that we feel it makes us vulnerable to non-disabled people turning round and saying – 'there you are then, we always knew that your lives were awful because of illness or incapacity, we always knew what a tragedy it is'.

In our discussions we reminded ourselves that one of the reasons we developed the social model of disability was to protect ourselves from the feelings of pity directed at us by non-disabled people who felt they had the right to tell us how we should feel about our experiences. In reality, such people were projecting their own fears of loss and pain, dependency and mortality onto us. In the process of defending ourselves from these onslaughts which undermined and disempowered us, which defined our lives as not worth living, there was little room for anything other than an assertion that it is external barriers, society's prejudice and discrimination, which disable us.

A number of women felt that the prominence of men within the disabled people's movement, and their general reluctance to talk about feelings, has made it difficult to move beyond this rather simplistic version of the social model. As one woman said, 'The emphasis has been on how it is society out there that disables us and we have developed a culture whereby we cannot talk about our individual pain and loss. It seems to me that we need to reclaim that it is okay to talk to each other about these things.'

As Liz Crow writes, we need to put back the experience of impairment into our politics. We need to write about, research and analyse the personal experience of our bodies and our minds for if we don't impose our own definitions and perspectives then the non-disabled world will continue to do it for us in ways which alienate and disempower us. Some of us have carried on talking about these issues and these discussions have influenced some of the contributions to this book. However, we do not feel that the public world, dominated by non-disabled people, is yet a safe place to fully share our experiences. While the personal experience of impairment and/or mental distress is relevant to most of the chapters in this book, there is a limit to which we can publicly explore this. In some ways, too, disabled women have found it easier to express grief, loss and pain – as well as strength and celebration – in the autobiographical and fictional writing to be found in books such as *Mustn't Grumble* (Keith, ed., 1994).

Feminism and Independent Living: a disabled woman's right to choose

While feminism can be interpreted in different ways and has various meanings, nevertheless, for most women, it is concerned with choice and control over our lives: a choice and control which is achieved by equal rights to housing, employment, education, equal status before the law, choice and control over sexuality and reproduction. It's also about feeling good about ourselves as women, recognising our worth and value in the contributions we make in every area of our lives.[1]

To many disabled people – men and women – all this will sound familiar, not so much because they associate these aspirations with feminism but because choice and control, and the rights and access necessary to attain these, are the independent living aims put forward by the disabled people's movement. Although we feel that neither feminism nor the disabled people's movement has adequately identified our concerns nor campaigned for the things that would make choice and control a real possibility for disabled women, we take our inspiration from both movements. Our insight and analysis of the oppression and injustice experienced by disabled women is informed and motivated by both feminism and disability rights.

This book deals with many of the key issues current in the debates within the disabled people's movement and feminism. It highlights the poor quality of education disabled children receive; the experiences of Black and Asian disabled women; the abuse experienced by disabled women and children; and women's experiences of the health and mental health systems. There are also ground-breaking analyses here of the social model of disability; of the public perceptions of disabled women; of the issues related by prenatal testing; and of the feminist perspective on 'caring'. We hope that this book makes a powerful contribution to the assertion of disabled women's strengths as autonomous, valued, human beings, and to the construction of a political and research agenda that increasingly reflects our concerns.

Notes
1 This paragraph reflects the thoughts of Alia Hassan, for whose thinking on independent living and feminism I am very grateful.

References
Barnes, Colin, ed., (1994) *Making Our Own Choices: Independent*

living, personal assistance and disabled people, British Council of Organisations of Disabled People.

David, M. (1991) 'Putting on an act for children?' in Maclean, M. and Groves, D., eds., *Women's Issues in Social Policy*, Routledge.

Keith, Lois, ed., (1994) *Mustn't Grumble: Writing by Disabled Women*, The Women's Press.

Kelly, Liz (1988) *Surviving Sexual Violence*, Polity Press.

Lloyd, Margaret (1992) 'Does she boil eggs? Towards a feminist model of disability', *Disability Handicap and Society*, Vol. 7, No. 3, pp. 207–21.

Lonsdale, Susan (1990) *Women and Disability*, Macmillan.

Morris, Jenny (1993) *Independent Lives? Community Care and Disabled People*, Macmillan.

Morris, Jenny (1995) 'Creating a space for absent voices: disabled women's experiences of receiving assistance with daily living activities', in *Feminist Review*, No. 51, pp. 68–93.

CHAPTER ONE

OUT OF SIGHT, OUT OF MIND:
The Experience and Effects of a 'Special' Residential School

Sally French

This chapter documents the experiences of eight visually impaired women, now in their forties, who spent their school days in a residential school for partially sighted girls in the 1950s and 1960s. Five of the women went to the school when they were five years old, one when she was six, and two when they were seven; they all remained at the school until they were 16. The interviews were semi-structured but the women were encouraged to expand freely. Some people who were approached to be interviewed found their experiences too painful to discuss and declined to take part. The women were all given pseudonyms to protect their anonymity, and for the purpose of this account they are: Gwen and Joy, who are sisters; Ruth and Celia, who are sisters; Andrea; Stella; Eve; Harriet.

The women give a powerful account of what life at the school was like, and the effect it has had on their lives. Only two of the women, Ruth and Andrea, had any experience of mainstream schooling. I spent four years at the school between the ages of nine and 13 and remember all of the women, though only three were in my immediate peer group.

The Barclay Institution
Barclay Home for Blind and Partially Blind Girls opened in Brighton in 1893. It was founded by a Mrs Campion with a

donation of £500 from a Mr Alexander Barclay, to teach industrial skills to blind and partially blind girls from workhouses and very poor homes. The Home was intended for young women of between 16 and 21 years of age, but almost from the start many of its inhabitants were children. The children of the Barclay Home received a very basic education and then joined the women in the 'technical school' where they continued to learn such crafts as basketwork and knitting. When one or more of these skills had been mastered, the women moved to the Barclay Workshops for blind and partially blind women where, for several years (or a lifetime) they eked out a meagre livelihood. In 1928 a shop was bought in Brighton to dispose of the goods they produced.

The Home grew very rapidly but over the years came to cater only for children. The school's philosophy remained focused on manual craft skills, and the expectations that the staff had of the children were low. The 1935 *Annual Report* stated:

> The aim is that a normal girl, leaving the Barclay Home at sixteen should be able, if required, to cut out and make a simple frock or child's garment, cook and serve a simple dinner nicely, be able to keep a house clean and orderly and, in addition, to employ her spare moments in making a basket or jumper.

Hurt (1988), in his history of special education, confirms that early institutions for blind and visually impaired people concentrated on training them in a number of manual crafts, and in so doing set a pattern for many years to come. Tomlinson (1982) points out that many of the early schools for blind and visually impaired children were founded by businessmen and were dominated by commercial interests.

In 1941, during the Second World War, the school was evacuated to a Queen Anne mansion (the former house of the Churchill family) in the Berkshire countryside where it remained until its closure in 1970; it is within this setting that all the women interviewed remember the school. Following the 1944 Education Act which, for educational purposes, separated blind and partially sighted children, the school was re-named 'Barclay School for Partially Sighted Girls'.

Memories of the first day

I asked the women I interviewed what they could remember of their first day at Barclay School and whether they understood what was happening to them. Eve, who went there just before her sixth birthday, had vivid memories:

> I can remember my parents telling me that I'd be going away to school but at the time I didn't realise I'd be living away from them on my own. They told me I'd be at school with lots of other children who wore glasses. I can remember Mum packing my case but I don't think I realised what was happening until I actually got to the school and into the gates. I saw this matron and my parents said goodbye to me and I think I realised then that they were going away and leaving me on my own and I panicked. I cried of course and got very upset; I remember saying to the matron 'I shall cry until I see my Mummy again.' I didn't see her again until we had a visiting day which was at least four weeks later. I know I was very upset and withdrawn for a while. I can remember the day I started there as if it was yesterday.

Joy had clear memories of her first day at the school too:

> I was absolutely longing to go because I had a sister there. I remember Mum naming all my clothes and getting everything ready, I was so excited – but when I'd been there half an hour I wanted to go home. I knew I'd got to stay there until I was 16 and when you're five that seems an eternity away. I can remember thinking how big it all was; living in a built-up area I'd never seen such a wide expanse of grounds before, they were kept lovely they really were – all the shrubberies, rhododendrons and daffodils. The first night in bed I can remember crying because I wanted to go home, and no one comforted you did they? No one at all . . . It was a long way from home and you didn't really have anybody.

There was nothing nice in the bedrooms either, no toys at all. I can remember my first day vividly.

Not all of the women understood why they were going to the school, or even that they were going until they were actually left on their own. Stella who went at the age of five, recalled:

I had no idea whatsoever that I was going to sleep there. As far as I was concerned I was going on a day outing and I'd be back at home by teatime, I had no idea that I was going to a special school, nobody explained it to me – I knew I was different from the rest of the family but I didn't understand why. When I got a bit older and I asked my parents why I had to go away, they just turned round and said it was because I was very special. That was it, I had to accept it.

Detachment from home and family

The women talked about how leaving home at such a young age made them feel about their families. Eve explained:

I didn't seem to feel like one of the family. I felt detached from them quite early on. I don't see a lot of my family now and I think the early separation is probably why. I remember my parents saying, a long time afterwards, that I was very withdrawn when they first took me out for a visiting day and that I didn't say anything to them unless they spoke to me first.

Stella also felt some degree of detachment from her family:

It wasn't that I didn't know them but I didn't know a family routine, that was the biggest problem. I also used to worry that I wouldn't recognise them when I was going home on the train, I used to think 'Will my Mummy know me?' and worry that I wouldn't find them on the station. But they would always call me and I would fly up the platform to them so excited. I didn't forget them.

Surprisingly, some of the women did not become detached

from their families. Andrea kept in close contact with hers, and even managed to keep the friends she had made during the one term she spent at the local infant school. She said:

> I was lucky, my parents came to see me as often as they could, it made all the difference, I felt as if they wanted me and I always felt part of the family. I had letters every week and they included me in everything that was going on. There were lots of people at home who knew me and they always greeted me when I came home. We lived in a small village where everybody knew everybody else (and everybody else's business). I used to correspond with my friends during the term and that helped a lot when I came home.

Harriet also kept in touch with the local children even though she had never been to school with them:

> It was a very tiny community-spirited village, we had Sunday School and Christmas parties and in the summer we had sports days on the village green. Everybody knew everybody and we all joined in. I didn't lose touch with it at all.

Education

The low expectations of the children and the emphasis on manual skills, persisted throughout the life of the school. In 1958, the year I arrived at the school, the *Annual Report* stated:

> It is recognised that many of the children will never reach a very high academic level, and this view is reinforced by the new Williams Intelligence Test for children with defective vision. We consider in consequence that a vocational bias is necessary at an earlier age and this is being introduced in the best possible way.

All of the women I interviewed remembered their education being dominated by domestic science and other practical skills. Joy recalled:

We had domestic science all day on Tuesdays and Thursdays. If we made a jelly we had to get the gelatine and the fruit juice, we couldn't just get a packet of jelly and pour boiling water on it. If we were weighing out we were made to do it without the scales, we had to use spoons. We used to make our own Christmas cakes and take them home, and Mrs Slater (the domestic science teacher) used to bring her husband's shirts in for us to iron. I enjoyed it, but the rest of the education was very bad. There was no 11-plus exam, there were no exams at all.

Stella recalled how the girls were taken out of their lessons for a week each year to spring clean the house, and how cleaning and domestic duties spilled over into other aspects of their lives:

I can remember doing housework before breakfast every day even on a Sunday, there was no excuse, everything had to be spick and span. We used to take a week out every year to spring clean the dormitories and playrooms. It was very hard, I can remember having to turn the mattresses over and brush them with a dustpan and brush, and getting on our hands and knees to do the skirting boards. It was all in school time. We used that awful thick wax polish on the floorboards. There was no excuse, every child had to do it.

The annual reports throughout the life of the school show that the majority of the girls, on leaving, worked in domestic service, factories, laundries, and as shop assistants and nursing auxiliaries. A small number gained employment in offices or received training in commercial skills. This pattern of employment is evident amongst the women I interviewed; on leaving school three worked in shops, one in a bakery, one as a nursing auxiliary, two in offices, and one in a factory. Andrea summed up their experience of education by saying,

I feel our education was very basic, they never gave us any opportunities or pushed us on to better things. Not many girls passed on to better schools, they could have done a lot more.

And Celia confirmed 'If your parents really insisted, you were allowed to sit the 11-plus but the education was too basic for many people to pass it.'

Very little money was spent on girls' education. In 1964, a typical year, £631 was spent on books, equipment, stationery, and educational visits (*Annual Report* 1964–65a). This can be compared with the sum of £1,233 which was spent on education at Blatchington Court, a school for partially sighted boys with a similar number of pupils (*Annual Report* 1964–65).

With few exceptions the teachers were remembered by the women as kind, non-threatening, and rather ineffective. Their failure to deal with the girls' needs arising from visual impairment is illustrated by Stella's experience:

I had a problem seeing to read the books but I would never admit to them because there was no such thing as 'can't' so I would struggle on regardless without seeing anything; in the seniors we didn't have any large print books. I was put in class two when I was small, it wasn't for mainstream children. All I remember doing was drawing and playing with toys. When I was moved after about two years I had missed a lot of the basics and I had a job to keep up. I had special reading lessons with the head teacher every playtime. I remember a word I got stuck on was 'ink'. It wasn't so much that I didn't know what the word was, it was that I couldn't see what it was, the letters looked joined up, but she couldn't understand that at all.

I can remember being made to play games, such as stool-ball, which few of us could manage, and going on endless nature walks where little of what was pointed out could be seen.

From 'sight saving' classes to contact lenses and low vision aids

The strong orientation to manual skills and crafts may, at least in part, have reflected ideas, prevalent until the 1940s, that people with severely defective sight must aim to 'save it' by refraining from any activity requiring close work. Before the Second World War, classes for partially sighted children were referred to as 'sight saving classes' where much of the teaching was oral. Corley et al. (1989) describe how children were compelled to work at arm's length wearing harnesses to prevent them from leaning forward. Their work was done on blackboards where writing of less than two inches in height was strictly forbidden. If pens were allowed, the nibs would be shielded to prevent the children seeing what they were writing; they even had to learn to write in that way.

These damaging ideas were slow to retreat. It was not until 1950 that the ophthalmologist of Barclay School states 'In conformity with present day views on myopia, we have relaxed considerably some of the more irksome restrictions, and I am informed that this has given rise to a marked psychological change.' (*Annual Report* 1949–50: p. 9).

Restrictions on activities such as reading and writing were replaced in the 1950s by a concentration on the development of contact lenses and various low vision aids; indeed the girls of Barclay School served as guinea pigs for many of these pioneering devices. In 1957 the ophthalmologist writes of his hopes that contact lenses 'will considerably improve not only their appearance and visual acuity, but also give them a greater sense of self-confidence' (*Annual Report* 1956–7: p. 13), and in 1960 he states 'It is gratifying to know that the work we have been doing at the Barclay School has been something of a pioneering effort.' (1959–60: p. 15).

Considerably less enthusiasm is shown for the contact lenses by Ruth and Celia, two sisters I interviewed, who were compelled to wear them. Ruth explained:

They expected you to cope and I didn't cope very well. I could wear them for a couple of hours but I was supposed to wear them for eight. I couldn't, my eyes wouldn't tolerate them although they did improve my sight. I had to sit there with them hurting and my eyes would be really blurry but there was no way I could take them out, nobody seemed at all sympathetic, the attitude was that you were lucky to be chosen. They weren't like modern contact lenses, they covered the whole eye, they were really thick and heavy. I don't know who paid for the wretched things but if you had them you were supposed to wear them because they were expensive. I suppose we were a group of young people with different eye conditions who they could try them out on. When I left I gave them up straight away, they were that uncomfortable.

Celia felt much the same:

They were really uncomfortable. I had a lot of problems and a lot of hassle at school because I used to find that the sun really played them up and I couldn't keep them in for as long as they thought I ought to. They wanted them to work because we were chosen and they definitely did improve my vision. They wouldn't let me take them out until I had had them in for the stipulated time so I had to sit there whether my eyes were streaming or not. I liked going to Moorfields though because we went on the train – I was only 10 or 11. As soon as I left I gave them up, I wear much smaller ones now.

Great excitement and enthusiasm for low vision aids is also expressed in the annual reports of this time, some of which contain deceptive photographs of girls reading from a 'normal' distance while using the aids. Relating an experience in the late-1950s of using telescopic lenses, I wrote:

I remember being photographed wearing the lenses by an American man whom I perceived to be very important. First of all he made me knit while wearing them, with the knitting held right down on my lap. This was easy as I could in any case knit without looking. He was unduly excited and enthusiastic and told me how much the lenses were helping. I knew he was wrong. Then he asked me to read, but this changed his mood completely; he became tense, and before taking the photograph he pushed the book, which was a couple of inches from my face, quite roughly to my knees.

Although I knew he had cheated and that what he had done was wrong, I still felt culpable for his displeasure and aware that I had failed an important test. (French, 1993: p. 71)

The daily routine

The accounts the women gave of the ways that they spent their time out of school hours give a picture of drudgery and regimentation. Andrea recalled:

In the summer we did the weeding, and in the autumn we had to clear up the leaves and twigs. On Saturdays we had to clean the house. We spent most of our time cleaning and doing things in the garden, it was all totally organised, we were all told what we were going to do whether we wanted to or not. It became a routine, a way of life and we just accepted it – what else could we do? We did the same thing week in, week out.

Eve had similar memories:

On a Saturday morning we had to weed the terraces with meat skewers. In the autumn we had to pick the leaves up off the lawn, every single leaf. We had to pick them up when it was frosty with our wet hands and they were freezing cold and mushy. We used to do that for a few hours until it was lunch time. Then we had to line up to wash our hands before lunch and use the one loo. If you didn't get a chance to go it was hard luck, you had to wait until afterwards. After lunch we went for a long walk in twos and we weren't allowed to look at anybody or talk to anybody who came along the road in the opposite direction. The matrons would say 'They don't want to talk to you, they don't want to see your ugly faces.' We then came back for tea and in the winter we'd have to read some library books. They weren't very interesting and some people couldn't see to read them. We went to bed at different times, the youngest ones at half past five and the oldest ones at half past eight.

Ruth remembered how heavy the work was:

We were allocated a room to clean every morning before breakfast. They had to be swept and dusted and the baths and loos cleaned. Then there was the ballroom and the squash court, I remember doing them on Saturdays – we did an awful lot of cleaning, heavy work. I remember big tins of polish, red it was, gungey stuff, and we had these big heavy things we called bumpers that we had to push up and down to polish the lino or the floorboards. After the meals we had to do the washing-up in big wooden sinks with really hot water and soda, and the job for Saturday evening was cleaning the shoes for Sundays.

This can be compared with the life-style of the Principal who, as well as having a personal maid (an ex-pupil of the school), occupied the finest rooms of the house.

Although some activities, like swimming, dancing, and musical appreciation, were enjoyed, none of the women could ever remember being given a choice about anything they did. Gwen recalled:

We used to play games on the grass when we were young, we had to go out. In the nice weather it was good but there was just the grass to play on, you had to make your own amusement and play your own games, you couldn't take toys out there except for balls and skipping ropes. You weren't allowed to take dolls or anything like that out there. I used to like the long walks because it got us out but you had no choice but to go and sometimes you didn't feel like it.

One of the duties of the older girls was to look after the smaller children. Andrea explained, 'When you became a prefect you had to sleep with the younger ones and look after them, you had to be there in the night if they needed you.' Gwen could remember being on a rota to help bath the little girls, she recalled:

We used to have to help with the bathing of them and putting them to bed. We had no choice but I didn't mind because it was something different. The little children used to like it when we rubbed them dry, they wanted someone to cling to because they were missing their parents. We had to clean their shoes and if your little one went off to church with dirty shoes you were told off.

Stella remembered the impersonal way in which they were compelled to treat the younger children:

We used to help bath the little ones and put them to bed, we were on a rota, it was one of the duties. We knew how to look after them but we weren't allowed to mother them, the matrons didn't like to see us getting friendly with them, they discouraged it.

All the women recalled total regimentation where every minute of their time was organised for them. Gwen explained:

It was very regimented, we had to queue up to have our shoes inspected, and when we had a bath we had to queue up to see that we were clean. All our time was organised for us, we didn't have to think for ourselves at all, we just had to do what we were told to do and that was life. We knew by the time of the day and by the bell what we had to do. We had to accept it, what else could we do?

Punishment and abuse

The care of the partially sighted places a special responsibility on the matrons and domestic staff, the warm thanks of the governors are due to them for the selfless way in which they fulfil their duties. (*Annual Report* 1959–60: p. 16)

The annual reports of Barclay School, like many official documents, give a false impression of what life was really like. Dr Connell, the school's physician comments, in 1945, on the good health of the girls, attributing it to 'Sister's unremitting care' (1944–45: p. 5), and Dr Chandler, a later physician, states 'I would like to take this opportunity of thanking Sister and her staff for the excellent care they have taken of the children this year' (*Annual Report* 1951–2: p. 13).

June Monkhouse, a pupil of the school from the age of eight to 11 in the early 1950s, writes about a frightening hair-brushing ritual she was forced to endure at the hands of Sister every night:

> After a few strokes she dug the brush in so hard and pulled it down my hair with such force, that it yanked my head right back, bringing a yelp of pain from me. 'Don't be such a baby' she snapped and continued to yank my head with every stroke. Each night after that she brushed my hair and I was terrified of her. (Monkhouse, 1980: p. 21)

She goes on to recall how Sister rapped her over the knuckles so hard that it made her chilblains bleed, forced her to clear up her own vomit when she was ill, and would 'whack my backside as hard as she could with a slipper'. She was severely reprimanded for being clumsy when she ran into a garden bench knocking out her front teeth, and recalls how, when she became distraught at the departure of her mother, she was segregated from the other children for her 'disgusting behaviour'. June states that 'even today I can say that she is the cruellest woman I have ever met.' (Monkhouse, 1980 p. 21).

Over the years the annual reports are no less congratulatory. In 1962 it is stated, 'it is once again my pleasure to express the sincere thanks of the governors to [the Principal] for yet another year of unsparing devotion to the welfare of the school as a whole and to the needs of each individual child' (*Annual Report* 1961–2: p. 12). This contrasts sharply with my own account of the school at this time when the abuse was no less evident:

> The matrons called us by our surnames and were very handy with rulers, wet flannels, skipping ropes, and their own physical force. They carried thick blue and white squared rulers and would lash out at the least offence; those with additional disabilities were frequent targets. I remember a five-year-old being subjected to this type of abuse

during her very first week at the school. The little girls slept
on the top floor and would have to walk downstairs in a
straight line keeping to the left; gaps in the line were a crime
worthy of punishment. This child, being uncertain of her
step in a strange place, allowed a gap to form in front of her
and the ruler was viciously lashed out. (French, 1992 p. 49)

All of the women I interviewed could remember harsh
punishments and an abusive psychological atmosphere. Stella
recalled:

Even as nippers we were made to stand facing the wall for
hours at a time. Quite regularly we would get the ruler
across the legs very hard. There might be no sweets for
weeks, or we were sent to bed without tea. Quite often
privileges like playtime were missed, instead we would have
to stand in the corner very straight. We often got stopped
from outings, I remember being stopped from a Christmas
party, we stood from half past two until six o'clock facing
the wall, there were about 12 of us that time. We were
marched out in front of the visitors and for tea we had
cheese and watercress while all the other children had fancy
cakes. The thing I did to deserve it was knocking the plants
over in the playroom when I was running around. I just
didn't see them but that wouldn't have been accepted, I was
thought to be careless and naughty. I knocked about three
plants over so I was banned from the Christmas party just
for that. It's vividly in my mind to this day.

Harriet recalled being grabbed by her hair, thrown across the
dormitory, and beaten with a wire coat-hanger by one of the
matrons. One of her earliest memories of life at the school was
a beating she received from the head matron who was a
qualified nurse:

We went to bed at half past five in the evening and we didn't
get up until seven o'clock in the morning, but we weren't
allowed to get out of bed to go to the toilet. I was very
unsettled because I'd gone to foster parents at the age of

three and then to school at the age of five, and one night I wet the bed. The prefect on duty realised what had happened and she tried to cover up for me, she got me out of bed and put me in the bath, but one of the matrons came along. She picked me up out of the bath, just as I was, soaking wet, and gave me the hiding of my life. It really hurt – you know what it's like when you're wet. I yelled and screamed, it terrified me.

Andrea, who on the whole was uncritical of the school, could remember at the age of six, being stood in the corner with her wet sheets tied around her neck, and later being made to wash them by hand.

Most of us shared the distressing memory of being prevented from going to the toilet when we needed to. Summing up this experience I wrote:

After tea we would all line up outside the loo on the ground floor; there were many others in the house of course but we had to be kept under constant supervision. During the entire evening, whether we were indoors or outside, we were not allowed to go so it was vitally important to take this opportunity, especially as there was often insufficient time before tea. How the matrons loved to humiliate us in this position; if we took more than a few seconds they were hammering on the door or barging in telling us to get a move on. Frequently they would send the back half of the queue away saying they were tired of seeing us jiggling around, that we had toilets on the brain, and that it was time we grew up and thought about something else for a change. (French, 1992: p. 20)

Most of the women had unpleasant memories of being forced, as very young children, to eat food they did not like, Celia recalled:

With any food you didn't like you were made to sit there. I don't like spaghetti and they put it in with the mince and I can remember sitting there until the middle of the afternoon whether it was stone cold or not, you were sat in the dining room when everybody else had gone back to school. When you got older if you were lucky enough to find someone who liked it you could pass it over without anybody seeing, but if you were caught you were given twice as much. I can remember some of the girls never got it down and were really heaving.

Stella remembered this treatment too:

What I hated was when they made you eat food that you didn't like. I hated Irish stew and they always made me eat it. I would be trying to get it down all through pudding and sometimes they brought it back at teatime. I was only five or six.

Joy felt particularly sad as she got older at the plight of the little children in the school, she explained:

None of us were comforted or even given a kind word. As we got older we could adapt to it but the little ones needed comfort and no one ever gave it to them. I didn't like them being ill-treated, I didn't like them being hit, they were away from home and they were unhappy. I saw it happen so much, I used to feel very sorry for the little kids when I got older.

Displays of emotion were always suppressed. Harriet and I both remembered how when a small girl learned of her Grandmother's death in a letter from home, she was told by the matron in front of us all, 'I could understand you crying if it was your mother, but you don't carry on like that when an old person dies.' The only place it was safe to cry was in bed, and even then it had to be silent.

All of the women recalled the behaviour of the matrons as being very cold and stern. Stella explained the effect this had on her:

There was never any affection or mothering not even when

you were five. Even when I was a little girl I didn't like sitting on my Mum's knee because I never got it at school. I became switched off from physical contact and couldn't cope with it. Friendships became very important, we leaned on each other a bit but we should have been able to approach the adults more. It was impossible, you couldn't go and confide in them, you couldn't tell them your little secrets or your little worries because it was frowned upon, they didn't want to be close to you, they were very Victorian in their attitudes towards children. They would often say we were appalling girls, always scruffy and untidy. We were made to think we were the lowest of the low. We were told off for the most simple things, a sock down was really frowned upon. I never ever remember them praising us for anything.

Eve recalled the psychological abuse she experienced and the effect this had on her:

There was too much discipline. They were ever so strict. They used to run people down all the time and make you feel that you were useless. They used to make you feel that you were there as a punishment rather than to learn anything. They didn't understand children at all, never mind their sight. They expected you to do what they wanted and they used to get really cross if you couldn't see something, or you couldn't clean your shoes properly, or do anything they wanted you to do; what confidence I had they took it all away. They were always shouting at us which made us frightened to speak up for ourselves, we didn't dare in case we got into trouble.

Harriet also recalled this treatment and the way she learned to cope with it.

They gave you the impression that you were at that school because you were some kind of delinquent. I was told that when I left school all I would be fit for was scrubbing out public lavatories; that was the kind of encouragement you had. But as I got older I found devious ways of sorting my life out so that it would be more pleasant. I used to volunteer for everything, then they would leave me alone, they weren't on my back all the time. But because I used to do this the other girls thought I was a creep and they used to make life very difficult. I started being hated by the kids but I could cope with that and I knew I couldn't have it both ways.

Those women whose parents lived near enough to visit, could remember that they were treated in a cold and distant way by the matrons as well. Joy explained:

They were more or less ignored, the matrons didn't converse with them. They didn't say 'Your daughter's got a problem' or 'Your daughter's upset about something'. They didn't bother about parents at all. If they got upset about parting with their daughters they just ignored them. I think it was terrible, there were no rights for parents at all.

Gwen had similar memories:

They were treated very coldly. They just came and took you out and brought you back, there was no cup of tea or anything like that. When they brought you back from a day out they had to go straight away, they couldn't linger around or come into the house.

Eve recalled how parents were criticised after they had left:

When we came back with our parents they'd be all nice while they were there, but as soon as they had gone they would criticise you and your parents. They would say that your parents weren't strict enough with you, that they shouldn't let you do 'this' or 'that', that you should be helping your parents more instead of running around the streets during the holidays. They seemed to think they treated us better than our parents did.

The abuse that the girls received led many to abscond from the school (Monkhouse, 1980). We could all remember how in

January 1960 two girls, aged 11 and 12, ran away in the night and were missing for two full days. They were found 100 miles from the school after receiving a lift from a lorry driver who sexually assaulted them many times (*Daily Express*, 30 January 1960; *Peterborough Citizen and Advertiser* 3 February 1960). The disappearance of the girls was kept from the press for 36 hours at the request of the Principal who was later accused of trying to preserve the reputation of the school at the expense of the children's safety (*Daily Express*, 28 January 1960). In answer to these accusations she stated, 'I have given 20 years of my life to these girls – how can it be said that I don't care?' (*Wokingham Times*, 5 February 1960). She goes on to say:

I love the children and of course they come first. I have devoted my life to them . . . There is nothing I could do to stop these children going away. This is a happy school. All the children are happy. (*Daily Mail*, 30 January 1960)

Although the girls were said to have recently been 'scolded' (*Daily Herald*, 29 January 1960) no enquiry of the school took place. In fact their behaviour was interpreted as a futile attempt to 'prove' to themselves that their partial sight was not a handicap (*Daily Mail*, 29 January 1960). They were returned to the school by the police as soon as they were found.

Telling parents
I asked the women if any of them had, as children, discussed the treatment they received at the school with their parents. Few of them had. Eve explained:

I didn't tell them anything. I don't know why I didn't, I think I just accepted it as normal. I suppose I thought that they wouldn't take any notice because if you reported anything at school nobody bothered, they'd just tell you to go away, or say 'it serves you right'. I suppose I thought there was no point telling adults about anything that happened to me. If you wrote a letter home you weren't allowed to tell your parents if you had been to the dentist or doctor or anything

like that. I thought all people were treated like that, I didn't
know any different. It wasn't until I left and went out into
the world that I realised how differently we had been
treated.

Stella's mother wouldn't take her seriously:

As I got older I felt very bitter. I told my parents what was
going on but my Mum used to say 'Well you must have been
naughty to deserve the punishment.' She wouldn't take it
seriously at all. My Mum's idea was that if you did
something wrong you got punished for it and that was it. I
don't think she realised how severely we were punished.

Joy and Gwen who are sisters told their parents very little. Joy
explained:

I thought it would worry them being so far away; even
when I was small I thought like that. I knew there was
nothing they could do, there was no way I could go home.
They knew I didn't like it but I didn't go into great detail
because it would only make them unhappy because they
didn't like being parted from us. I knew if I told them things
it would make everything worse.

Confiding in parents during term time was prevented by the
matrons and the regime of the school. No telephone calls were
allowed and letters were carefully censored. Stella recalled:

On Sunday we had letter writing after church, all the letters
were read and if the matrons didn't like them they would rip
them up and tell us to write them again. It happened to me
when I said I wasn't very happy or when I moaned that I'd
been told off. It happened to a lot of children quite regularly.

Adolescence
Most of the women recalled a total lack of privacy at the school
which they found more difficult as they reached adolescence.
Joy explained:

I didn't like the way we were all in the bathrooms together, as you got older it wasn't nice. There was one in the bath, one drying, and one waiting. There was always four or five girls in the bathroom at the same time. The matrons were in and out too, nobody was trusted to bath themselves, nobody was trusted at all.

Ruth had similar memories:

There was a total lack of privacy, you were all together in these big rooms, all got dressed together, all in the bathrooms together. Even the toilets had no locks on the door, you had to sit there and yell 'Somebody's in' right up until you were 16.

Stella recalled how they were inspected after bathing:

We had to queue up waiting for a bath, there was never any privacy. They even used to (I don't like to say this) make us stand in our pyjama bottoms and lift our arms up to check that we had washed everywhere. They were very strict about it. That was when we were 15 or 16.

Harriet found lack of privacy so much a part of normal life that she had to learn to be private:

There was no privacy whatsoever. It got to the stage that when you got home you forgot about privacy and you would start undressing in front of people or in the wrong place. Nobody worried about somebody standing naked in front of them at the school and I thought that was the way things were, I didn't know any different. It took me a long time to learn about privacy and to learn how to be private.

The women recalled how they were made to dress very plainly in clothes that were nearly always old. They became particularly conscious of this during adolescence. Stella recalled:

They frowned upon make-up and I never remember

wearing tights or stockings at school. We used to wear awful grey socks and black outdoor shoes even with our own dresses right up until we were 16. They didn't like us having fancy hair styles, it was always commented on. I was lucky as I have naturally wavy hair so I could get it into a reasonable style. They wanted us to look very plain. Everything was passed down, you were lucky to get anything new. The shoes were awful, only once do I remember getting a new pair and I thought I was the bee's knees in them.

Andrea remembered the old clothes too and that they only had clean clothes once a week:

You thought you were the bee's knees if you got a new jumper that nobody else had worn. A lot of them were old and darned, I never had a brand new one. I did get a new pair of shoes once but mostly they were handed down. The thing that really got me most was having to wear the same pair of knickers all week. We only got clean clothes once a week even when we were teenagers. We used to wash them out at night and dry them on the radiators, but even then they'd ask you why.

None of the women could remember having menstruation explained or having any sex education. Ruth recalled:

When you got a bit older you saw the girls going to this special drawer on the landing, that was where they kept the sanitary towels. We had to tell the matron and there was this special toilet we had to use. If it started unexpectedly then that was your hard luck because you had one clean pair of knickers a week and that was it, they wouldn't give you another pair.

Stella remembered being kept in total ignorance:

They didn't explain about your periods other than it was something that happened to every young woman. My mum was also that way. Even when it was happening I didn't know what it was all about.

The demise of Barclay School

A year before Barclay School closed an inspection took place where 'much useful advice was given' (*Annual Report* 1967–8: p. 5) A CSE stream was established and specialist teachers in Mathematics, English, History, and Geography were employed. It is stated that 'This arrangement is working well; it gives the girls an incentive to work and to achieve what is done in the ordinary Secondary Modern School' (*Annual Report* 1967–8: p. 5). But a year later, in 1969, Barclay School amalgamated with Blatchington Court School for Partially Sighted Boys in Seaford; two of the matrons transferred with the girls (*Annual Report* 1970–71). The reasons for the amalgamation are unclear, but it was probably due to a dwindling number of pupils on roll.

The beautiful Queen Anne mansion is now an outstanding hotel. Its glossy brochure says that 'Over the years, this magnificent building has assumed an assortment of prestigious guests' (The Royal Berkshire, undated). No mention is made of the many girls who, for 20 years, were confined and abused within its gates.

The effects of Barclay School

A lack of confidence
Most of the women left Barclay School with debilitating feelings about themselves which took many years to reduce or subside. Eve said:

> I don't feel as self-confident as I should do really, although I've got better as the years have gone on. I went on an assertiveness training course which helped. Even now I sometimes find it hard to think for myself, just ordinary, everyday, silly things. I feel almost ashamed of being partially sighted too. I think it's because of the school, they undermined your confidence all the time, I think it will always be with me a bit.

Gwen had similar feelings:

> You gain confidence as the years journey on. At one time I couldn't stand up to anyone but I can now. You lack confidence becuase you have never been allowed to think for yourself, and then suddenly you have to, and it's hard. I didn't form opinions, I didn't really need to, everything in life was done for me. It makes you lazy and it's hard when you leave school because you are waiting all the time to be told what to do. I got a lot of help from my parents but I was very late developing.

Harriet suffered a debilitating lack of self-esteem too:

> The most damaging thing was the way they destroyed your self-confidence. The way they said that you couldn't do things because you were 'such and such' a person or because of your background. They really put you down. When you went out into the world you weren't your own person you were what they said you were. You had it drummed into you all the time 'you're a delinquent, you're no good for anything.' It made you feel you had to keep in the background all the time because you weren't as good as other people – I used to feel 'I'm nothing, I'm nobody, I can't do it.' But I gradually found that I could.

Most of the women were frightened of travelling and going out on their own because they had never been permitted to do so. Stella recalled:

> I was frightened to go out to be honest because I hadn't even been shown how to get on a bus. I didn't make any friends for four or five years because I was too frightened to go out on my own. If I did I would drive my Mum potty asking her over and over again 'Where will the door be?', 'When will the bus come?' I didn't have the confidence to find anything out for myself, I had to know every single detail before I would go anywhere. It wasn't until I was over 20 that I started going out socially.

Harriet had similar difficulties:

> I had no confidence whatsoever. The first day I went out on my own was the day I started work. I had to walk a mile to the bus stop and when I got half way there I started panicking, I was thinking 'Say if I get on the wrong bus?' 'Say if I land up in the wrong town?' I had to stand still for a few minutes and pull myself together. I was very timid and very nervous.

Stella still finds it hard to ask for the help she needs which she believes stems from the attitudes of the staff at the school:

> At school we were always told 'There's no such thing as 'can't' – we weren't allowed to say we couldn't see things. I find it very hard to ask for help or to admit that I need a bit of assistance.

Most of the women felt socially inadequate when meeting people for some years after leaving school. Stella explained:

> I was very nervous of meeting people, I didn't know how to approach them. I couldn't talk to them because all the time I was at school it was always 'yes thank you' and 'no thank you', there were no 'ifs' or 'buts' about anything. There was never any conversation with adults at school so I didn't know how to approach them. Even now I find it difficult at times, I still feel apprehensive of people in authority and I have awful problems making decisions. It is purely lack of confidence because we were never allowed to think for ourselves. Eventually you have to fight back and get on with it. I met a young chap who was very good to me and that set me up with going out a bit. It was very hard but I realised I had to be more positive. I had to fight against my parents too because they were very protective.

Eve's experiences were similar:

> I was very quiet. We were brought up in school not to talk to

other people unless they spoke first – they drummed that into you – so I didn't make friends very easily. I didn't know anybody and I felt different from everybody else. I was very lonely for the first few years but I got more confident as time went on. When I worked at Waitrose I met this girl, Pat, who was partially deaf so we had something in common, both having a disability. She had a lot more confidence than me and she used to say 'let's do this' and 'let's do that' and we did. She helped me quite a bit. My husband is very supportive too, whatever I want to do he backs me up like anything, he's helped me to build up my confidence.

Harriet's self-confidence did not really improve to any great extent until she had her first guide dog in 1982:

I was afraid of people, if anybody said my name a bit sharply I would jump and think I had done something wrong. I was really scared, I used to go right into my shell and cry and tremble. I hardly ever used to speak to anybody, my foster parents wouldn't let me bring anybody home so that didn't help. It was having a guide dog that brought me out of myself. People started talking to me because I had the dog and I gradually learned to relate to them. The dog opened all sorts of doors. If somebody had told me 12 years ago that I would be able to stand up and talk to a room of over a hundred people without even thinking about it then I would have laughed at them. But today I do it and I can't believe I'm doing it. I go to seminars and conferences, I've even tutored at seminars. I had no idea I was capable of it, I thought I was stupid and dim. The dog has made so much difference to my life that I can't start to tell you. I feel I can tackle most things now whereas before I felt as if I couldn't tackle anything, I felt useless.

These feelings of shyness and inadequacy were compounded by the fact that some of the women had become detached from their home communities. Ruth explained:

I didn't know anybody, we lived outside a village and there

was nobody of my own age, it was very hard. It was such a different environment from school and I was very, very shy. I got friendly with a girl in the toy shop though and we used to go about together and that helped.

Eve went to a vocational college run by the Royal National Institute for the Blind when she left school. It is ironic that she needed the services of one blindness institution to combat the effects of another. Eve explained:

It was the complete opposite of Barclay because they tried to bring out the best in you and to teach you how to cope in the outside world. If I hadn't been there I don't know how I would have got on. We went out on our own which was another thing I had never been allowed to do at school, we had to do mobility tests. Even in the holidays I didn't go out by myself very much because I had no practice and I was worried. It was the complete opposite of Barclay.

Home, men, and children

Some of the women commented on the effect of growing up in an all female environment. Stella said:

It had a devastating effect on me, I certainly didn't know how to approach the boys. I've been out with men sometimes but I've never really stuck with any of them, I feel happier with women. Men are like another species to me, it definitely stems back to those days.

Joy recalled:

It had a terrible effect, I didn't have a clue what to do when I went out into the world. In my first job I worked as a ward orderly which I loved, I left school one week and I was there the next and I kept thinking 'Please let it be a female ward' – I don't think I could have coped with a man, never mind a man with no clothes on! Anyway, it was a female ward and I was treated very well there and later I looked after the men, and I got used to it. But as far as relationships and friends were concerned it was very hard indeed.

Although Eve had become detached from her family at a young age, she succeeded in making a happy home for her husband and children:

I always thought that when I had children I wouldn't want them to go through what I went through. I wanted to give them as much love as I could. My parents wondered how I'd manage with children, but I did. I think a lot of it is common sense. I remember when I was expecting my daughter the first thing my dad said was 'How will she manage?' He didn't say he was pleased or anything like that.

Ruth and Andrea have children with visual impairments, and Celia has a daughter with cerebral palsy causing severe physical disabilities and learning difficulties. Ruth's daughter went through mainstream school and managed well, but Andrea's son and Celia's daughter went to special schools. Celia explained:

I didn't want her to go away to boarding school. Fortunately in this area there are some very good special day schools so Lucy was lucky she got into one. But later we were offered a partial residential place because the caring was very hard, she was getting bigger and I had a son by them. Now she is grown up and lives in an ordinary house with five other young women. There was no way she could go to an ordinary school.

Andrea had mixed feelings about the education of her son:

I think it did him good to mix with other children and to have the insight of knowing what an ordinary school was like, but he said himself that he didn't want to go to the local secondary school. I don't think he would have got the help that he needed there, his reading was quite bad before he went away to school, but in a year it was the standard it should have been for his age. In hindsight I wonder whether he'd have been better off going to that school at five or six. I always told him that if he wasn't happy anywhere he wouldn't have to stay, I didn't want him to suffer the way I did.

Employment

All of the women believed that their employment chances had been severely hindered by the education they had received. Gwen said:

I've been happy with the jobs I've had but you don't feel confident to go for the job you want because you haven't got the scholarship you need. The education you got there was just enough to get you by.

Stella had similar feelings:

I was well-prepared for work in the bakery, I was good at it but I didn't enjoy it. It was very hard, very long hours. It wasn't what I would have chosen but I wasn't educated to a high enough standard to go for anything else.

Eve felt it was lack of confidence, as much as a poor education, which caused her to be reticent when looking for work or applying for jobs. Overall the women were, however, happy with their present work and the work they had had in the past. Joy said:

I enjoyed working in the hospital, I was there for six years. I then trained in switchboard work, and now I work in Marks and Spencer in the food section which is very good. All the work I have done I have thoroughly enjoyed.

Celia has similar feelings:

I started work in the Delicatessen and stayed there for four or five years. Then I worked in the local post office where we lived in the village, serving the customers and working in the shop. I've been happy enough, but at times I think perhaps I could have done better.

Conclusion

Unless it be thought that this account gives a purely historical view – focusing on the 'olden days' when people knew no better – it is important to realise that disabled children, including those in institutions, are still more likely to suffer abuse than their non-disabled peers (see *The ABCD Pack* and Margaret Kennedy's chapter in this book). Camblin (1982) concluded, from a review of the literature, that children who are viewed as 'different' or 'difficult' are more likely to be abused than other children, and Westcott (1993), in her interviews with disabled people, uncovered considerable physical, emotional and sexual abuse. It can also be seen that long-term incarceration can have profound and lasting effects on those subjected to it. Stella summed up what many women said about the effects of Barclay School on their lives:

> I don't think you ever get over something like that 100 per cent. But having said that as long as you can earn your living, have a nice home, and be independent then your life is not a failure, but there's a cloud hanging over you because you can remember a lot of bad things.

It is a tribute to the women that they emerged from this experience capable and warm human beings.

This account validates our experiences as visually impaired women and has brought to light the cruelty which existed in blindness institutions in the very recent past. Disabled people are now speaking out and the widespread belief that they are not abused is finally being dispelled (see Baker 1990, Potts and Fido 1991, Humphries and Gordon 1992, Atkinson, ed., 1993). But there are still many more voices to be heard and stories to be told.

References

ABCD Consortium (1994) *The ABCD Pack: Abuse and children who are disabled* (1993) ABCD Consortium (c/o NSPCC Child Protection Training Group).

Annual Reports, Barclay Home for Blind and Partially Blind Girls, 1928–45.

Annual Reports, Barclay School for Partially Sighted Girls, 1948–68.

Annual Reports (1964–65; 1970–71). Blatchington Court School for Partially Sighted Boys.

Atkinson, D., (1993) *Past Times: Older people with learning difficulties look back on their lives*, Open University Press.

Baker, M. (1990) *With All Hopes Dashed in the Human Zoo*, Danny Howell Books.

Camblin, L.D. (1982) 'A survey of state efforts in gathering information on child abuse and neglect in handicapped populations,' in *Child Abuse and Neglect*, Vol. 6, No. 4, pp. 465–72.

Corley, G., Robinson, D. and Lockett, S. (1989) *Partially Sighted Children*, NFER – Nelson.

French, S. (1992) 'Memories of School – 1958–1962' in O'Keefe' S., ed., *Living Proof*, Royal National Institute for the Blind.

French, S. (1993) '"Can You See the Rainbow?" the roots of denial', in Swain, J., Finkelstein, V., French, S. and Oliver, M. *Disabling Barriers – Enabling Environments*, Sage.

Humphries, S. and Gordon, P. (1992) *Out of Sight: The experience of Disability 1900–1950*, Northcote House.

Hurt, J.S. (1988) *Outside the Mainstream*, B. T. Batford.

Monkhouse, J. (1980) *Sight in the Dark*, Hodder and Stoughton.

Nicholls, S. (1989) 'A day in the life of . . .', *The New Beacon*, Vol. 73, No. 868, pp. 304–5.

Potts, M. and Fido, R. (1991) *A Fit Person to be Removed: Personal accounts of life in a mental deficiency institution*, Northcote House.

The Royal Berkshire (undated), *Hotel Brochure*.

Tomlinson, S. (1982) *A Sociology of Special Education*, Routledge & Kegan Paul.

Westcott, H. (1993) *Abuse of Children and Adults with Disabilities*, NSPCC.

CHAPTER TWO

A STRANGER IN MANY CAMPS:
The Experience of Disabled Black and Ethnic Minority Women

Ayesha Vernon

Introduction

This chapter concerns the education and employment experience of Black and ethnic minority disabled women and is based on a small qualitative piece of research. For many feminist researchers, their personal history is an important part of why and how they approach their work. I am no exception; my research subjects' experiences of education and employment are also my experiences and it is inevitable that this will inform my perspective. I will therefore start by giving a brief account of my personal history.

I was born in a rural village in the state of Gujerat in south-west India where the main means of income was farming. I was the third child in the family after a much coveted first boy and then a girl. By then, my father had married three women and had a child from each of them and I was the child of his third wife. My father divorced my mother when I was less than two years old, and I was separated from her. This was because it was customary that the man keeps the children, thus leaving the woman free to marry again.

It was difficult for my family to eke out a living by farming the acre of land that we had so my father went to Africa for economic reasons leaving me and my half brother with my grandfather and step grandmother. My grandmother had a severe form of arthritis and found it difficult to cope with us so

I was sent to my aunty's house in another village, who also had several children of her own. It was while I was staying there that I became very ill as a result of which I became blind. It was very sudden and we now think that it was meningitis.

My blindness came as a dreadful shock to my family. They thought that it would have been better if I had died, instead of being a burden to them. My being blind was thought especially a tragedy because I was a girl. If I had been a boy, it would have been a lot easier as they would have found a sighted wife to look after me and I could have still fulfilled my role as a father and a husband. For a blind woman, there was nothing to be done except to hope for a cure. I would not be able to marry a sighted man or a blind man, as it was thought impossible for me to be able to fufil my womanly role of wife and mother. My neighbours and my family often said that if I had been a boy, it would not have been half as bad; as a girl it would have been better to let me die, since my life would not be worth living.

My grandfather looked after me until I was 14 years old. Throughout my childhood, he searched for a cure for my blindness. Much of the treatment I received was based around religion, and it was often said to me that the only reason I was not getting better, was because I did not want to get better. At the age of 14, my father came back to India to remarry and take his family with him to England as he had been working there for the previous five years. Thus, I came to England with him and had my first opportunity for education.

I spent six years in two residential institutions for the blind and three years in a mainstream higher education college. These nine years away from home and from the tyrannical rule of my father played a crucial role in my liberation.

My father regretted ever letting me leave his house to be educated. There was no way he could find me a partner through arranged marriage, but he did not want me to work and have a career because he did not see that to be a woman's role. He just wanted me to stay at home and sit in a corner to vegetate. I know that if I had been a man he would have been very proud of my achievements and would have encouraged me. He finally disowned me when I married a man of my own choice.

My experience of racism started when I went to my first residential school for the blind which was all white apart from myself and an Asian boy. There I experienced physical and verbal abuse from the children and less favourable treatment from some of the staff. I could hardly speak any English, I wore Indian clothes and as a Muslim I needed a special diet. Gradually and in subtle ways, I was persuaded to wear English clothes and eat English food. The staff promised that they would not tell my father about it. I had to eat the food. If I hadn't I would have starved because the only alternative they would give me was salad. On one occasion they put a plate of sausages in front of me. I knew what it was by its smell. When I asked the housemother why I had sausages on my plate she snatched it from me and said 'go without then!' That day I didn't eat anything. The staff kept giving me other people's secondhand clothes to wear as I could not buy any of my own. I had to wear the clothes to survive and be accepted. Of course, my taking on an English identity did not stop the racist comments from other children, because I could not change my skin colour.

My experience of being both disabled and Black was truly brought home to me when, on my first day at a mainstream college of higher education, the warden of the residential hall where I was staying said 'You have a double handicap in that most people have never met a coloured or a blind person, let alone a coloured blind person.' The implication was that I should not expect to make any friends. This immediately made me feel an outcast. I was the only disabled student among 5,000 students and there were only a handful of Black students. That night I nearly packed my bags and went home. But I stayed as the alternative of going back to the tyrannical rule of my father and vegetating in a corner was too grim to contemplate. Before that fatal comment which dashed my confidence to pieces in a flash, I had already met and thought I had made some friends, but after that I kept myself to myself and focused my attentions on my studies which I saw as the key to my liberation.

Although the degree was based on social policy and race relations, i.e. oppression, my experience as a disabled person was not recognised by either the lecturers or the students. So while the degree covered issues around race and gender, it was not until I left the college that I discovered the social model of disability and a whole movement around disability issues. I rejoiced heartily at discovering a movement that expressed my experience of disability as an oppression, but I still found it lacking in that it did not acknowledge my experience as a disabled Black woman which is totally different from that of a disabled white man.

In employment I have experienced disablism, racism, and sexism. My first job was at a major charity for disabled people where I experienced overt and blatant racism from my white supervisor who praised my work one week and the next decided that I ought to retake the test that I had passed with flying colours. In the end, she dismissed me, with the excuse that my English was not good enough. From there I went to work in a Black organisation to promote race relations. Here I found that my being disabled made me an outcast from other Black colleagues. I also experienced a very crude form of sexual harassment from one particular individual.

My experience as a disabled woman within the Black community is very challenging for some Black people. In the past, I have been warned not to voice the disablism of the Black community for fear of portraying Black people in a bad light and provoking racism. I think that far from provoking racism, Black people would do well to acknowledge their own prejudices, for until you truly learn to judge yourself, you cannot judge others. This is not to deny the role of racism in Black people's lives and its harmful effects, but Black people are victimisers as well as being victims of oppression. The same is also true of women and disabled people – the fact that someone is oppressed does not mean that they are free of prejudices against other oppressed groups in society. Until Black people in the fight against racism, women in the fight against sexism and disabled people in the fight against disablism fully acknowledge their own prejudices towards other oppressed minority groups, they are denying a significant part of disabled Black men and women's experiences and doing little to further their own causes. For, as long as we are divided and fighting our own exclusive causes, we will continue to be oppressed.

There is little known about the experiences of Black disabled women. There is particularly little research and writing from our point of view. This chapter is an attempt to start to give voice to our experiences. It is based on 10 in-depth semi-structured taped interviews with disabled Black and ethnic minority women, and concerns their experiences in education and in gaining paid employment. Two of the women are Indian, one is East African Asian, three are Pakistani, three Afro-Caribbean and one woman is Arabian. The ages of the women range from 25 to 38, with three women in their mid to late twenties and the rest in their early to mid-thirties. Seven of the women are single with no children, one is a single parent, one married with children and one married without children.

The interviews were transcribed into written print, a copy of which was sent back to the women in an accessible format for them to reflect and comment on in any way they wished. To make it fully accessible to all the women concerned, they were given the option either to send the amended transcript back to me or phone their comments to me which I was able to take down on the computer as they dictated. I was then able to amend their transcript accordingly and send back to them the amended version for them to keep. They were asked to choose their own pseudonym.

In an attempt not to exploit and alienate the women I was able to share my own experiences with them, which helped to promote a feeling of mutual understanding and trust between us. My life has been enriched by sharing such intimate experiences with these women and by witnessing the sheer strength of spirit and determination with which they fought their numerous daily battles in order to live their lives.

I am deeply grateful to these women for sharing their traumatic struggles and triumphant achievements with me. Five of the women interviewed are still in regular contact with me to discuss strategies such as assertiveness and interview techniques.

The meaning of work

Employment is the means to life. It enables our physical survival as well as being a key determinant of our sense of mental well-being. As we enter adulthood, work is a crucial means of gaining emotional and economic independence. This is no different for disabled people; in fact, work may be particularly important as a way of offsetting disabling attitudes and situations which undermine self-esteem and hamper our independence.

Shafeen certainly feels that work has helped her to over-come the low self esteem created by the onset of her disability and others' attitudes to it: 'I do take my work very seriously. My work definitely helps with my self esteem. Since I started this job, the responsibility has really made me much more confident as a person.' She identified that her previous lack of confidence was related to her dependence on her parents. 'I have been quite dependent on my parents since my accident because I live with them and I find this dependency extremely unhealthy. It has affected me psychologically. So work is very important, as a disabled person and as a woman, because I am independent at work and because it gives me opportunities and ways to perform that I didn't have before. It gives me confidence and raises my self-esteem and it is helping me to come to terms with my disability.'

Shazia too feels that work is a big part of her identity and independence and that this is especially important because she is a woman and disabled: 'For me work gives me identity. Obviously, as a woman, economic independence is really important and in terms of my disability I need that inde-pendence.'

For some disabled women, like Neelam, employment is the only thing which stops them being virtual prisoners in their own home with no sense of what the outside world is like. As Neelam explained, 'It has given me a bit more realisation as to what the world outside is like. I would not have had any knowledge of that if I was unemployed. I would mostly have sat in the house but had no knowledge of the outside world.'

Shazia talked about how satisfaction and fulfilment in her work is crucial to her happiness: 'For me if I am not happy in my job I am not a happy person . . . At work there is a sense of not being isolated, a sense of learning, developing, of giving, a sense of achievement. I can go home on a real high. Work is a big part of everybody's life and if you don't have access to work then part of you isn't going to develop.'

Other women talked about their need to have a sense of purpose and how work gave meaning to life for them. For Momta employment means several things: 'Financial security is one factor, money to fulfil personal plans in the present and for your future. That's the first thing. And, secondly, for self pride really, to feel that you are actually achieving something out there. In terms of disability I feel that I am achieving quite a lot. Dignity comes into it as well, because we are not supposed to work. As disabled people we are not expected to earn our own living. We are supposed to be dependent and looked after.'

Paid work is a way of determining our social status. For example, Neelam felt that to be employed was crucial to her gaining a place in the world: 'There is a great deal of status in being employed. People respect you. People think you are part of the world, a part of society in a sense. Whereas, when you are unemployed you have no status, you have nothing, you are seen and treated as a nobody. It definitely gives you status and in some sense that has given me confidence.'

Indeed, paid work is deemed so important that women's work in the home, even though it is often for longer hours and more demanding than paid work, is not acknowledged as 'work'. 'Work' gives people a place in the world, a part in society. It defines who we are. This is evident in the fact that 'what do you do?' is usually the first question that people ask when they get chatting with a stranger. They don't mean what do you do at home or in your leisure time, but what do you do in paid employment. The question implies, what is your position in society? And the answer seems immediately to give people an idea of the other person's standard of living, intellectual ability, educational level and social standing.

It is for gainful employment that we spend the first 16 to 20 years or more of our life in education. We are preparing for 'work'. Yet disabled people are not expected to work because the general assumption is that we are not capable of working.

So how does this attitude – combined with expectations about women's role within the family – affect disabled women's experience of education? And to what extent does racism impinge on Black and ethnic minority disabled women's experience of schooling?

Education – a preparation for life?
Good and equal education is vital in preparing people for life's opportunities. However, disabled Black and ethnic minority women's experiences indicate that they do not have access to equal education. There are many factors involved.

Seven of the women interviewed had attended a special (i.e. segregated) school, although of these, five had also at some point in their primary or secondary education been sent to a mainstream school. Eight of them had received some form of further or higher education, and for two of these this had been at a segregated establishment.

At special schools there is often a focus on things like physiotherapy which some women felt had a negative effect on their education. Momta, who came to Britain at the age of 12 from Uganda, found that her education suffered because of a focus on medical and rehabilitation needs. 'At the top of everybody's priorities was the physical side. You know, get you on your feet and get you moving was the most important thing in special school. Like swimming and physio was more important than the actual study side. There was a lot of disappointment as far as I was concerned. I had expectations of a good level of education here that I could have gained to make up for lost time. In special school we just did basic English and maths which I was already way beyond anyway, so I didn't gain anything by going to a special school.'

A focus on trying to get disabled children to do what is considered to be 'normal' can get in the way of education. Sunita first went to a school for deaf children but her father didn't want her to use sign language so she was moved to a mainstream school with a partially hearing unit where there was no sign language provision. She had long daily sessions of speech therapy. Her education suffered because the emphasis was on getting her to speak 'normally'. 'I feel education is more important and my younger brother used to pick on me, saying

I had very easy work at school. I should have had the same education as the hearing people.'

Most of the women who went to special schools felt that their education was of a lower quality than it should have been. Laila spoke about her experience of segregated education: 'it didn't prepare me at all, it was a nightmare really . . . They didn't want me to do anything. They had very low expectations of me.'

Mary also felt that her education in a segregated all-white school did not enable her to maximise her potential. 'You are over protected in special schools. I found that unless you were really clever, they never really gave you a chance.' Like many children who attend segregated schools, Mary felt as if 'I had already been written off.'

Restricted choices were also experienced in segregated further education. After leaving school Momta went to a segregated further education college where she 'did a business studies course, RSA, which has no value now. But that was the only thing that was on offer.'

Sometimes, however, the particular facilities available at a segregated school or college can make education more accessible than in a mainstream setting where there is often little attention paid to the particular needs of children with, for example, sensory impairments. Anita, who is deaf, had a difficult experience of primary education because she was in a mainstream school with no facilities for deaf children. As she explained: 'From the age of five to 11 I lost out on all my education because I was in a class with 40 hearing pupils and one teacher and I could not function at all in that environment. There was one peripatetic teacher who used to read to me which I never understood. So by the time I was 11, I was behind all my peers and I hadn't got basic reading, writing or arithmetic skills at all.' Anita was labelled a 'slow learner': 'They thought I was backward with a learning difficulty. It was actually the environment. They did not cater for my needs.' At the age of 11 Anita was sent to a segregated school for deaf children against her parents' wishes. However for Anita it proved to be, 'one of the best years of my life. I made progress by leaps and bounds . . . it was the best thing that could have happened to me because it was right for my needs at that time. The residential school had a loop system and you wore headphones and for the first time I heard sound. Before that I wasn't speaking properly, I was not communicating. At this special school I made progress with my spoken English overnight and with other subjects. I was taught orally but I also had access to BSL which I picked up very quickly.'

All of those who attended a mainstream school found there were barriers to their education and these often resulted in assessments that they were not able to 'cope' and should be sent to a special school. Sometimes these barriers were the material ones of lack of facilitation to meet the needs arising from their impairment (such as sign language interpretation, brailled or taped material, access to all parts of the school); often there were also attitudinal barriers. A failure of mainstream schools to understand and respond to the needs created by impairment means that, like Anita, many children with physical and/or sensory impairments are at risk of being categorised as having learning difficulties as well. Jackie, for example, was also labelled 'a slow learner': 'Because they never took time with me I was pushed into special schools. I think if I had had the support I would have been in mainstream schools. I was slow reading and writing. If you are not one of those who is bright you are finished.'

A failure to take account of needs arising from physical/ sensory impairment was not confined to schools. Neelam talked about the indirect discrimination that she experienced at the higher education institution she attended: 'They wouldn't give me the book list in advance. If they had done this I could have sent it to the RNIB and they would have put the books on tape for me. But I ended up having to have the books read out to me by my reader. So I ended up going to the book shop and getting my reader to read to me.' Unless proper provision is made to meet needs arising from impairment, it is difficult to see how children and young people can reach their full potential.

For Black and ethnic minority children, racism can sometimes get in the way of how abilities are assessed. Jackie explained how, 'The psychologist came and did this test on me.

In those days, everybody believed in them and trusted them so I went to a special school.' The psychologist's test included what utensils Jackie used to eat her food. She was supposed to have used a fork, instead she used a spoon. 'We have rice and peas for which we use a spoon. Some people use their hands and some use spoons, that's their culture. I don't know what they were going on about, all I know is that after that I went to a special school. That was a downfall for me because I knew that there was nothing positive about the school. My mum didn't have any say really because you believed the psychologists in those days.' At the school Jackie felt that, 'There was nothing positive about black people in books or in anything else, it was all about white people and what they had done.' Jackie felt she was barred from making any academic progress. 'It was the attitude, you people with learning difficulties, how can you take exams?'

Being isolated as the only Black or Asian child can create difficulties. Mary felt that her education suffered both from being in a segregated school and from the fact that she was the only Black child there. 'You are over protected in special schools . . . They didn't give me any encouragement. It was as though I was already written off . . . Their attitude was, oh you'll never get anywhere and I think it was because I was Black. I was the only Black person in the school.'

Neelam, too, experienced problems as the only Asian girl at her school for blind girls. 'They had no knowledge in terms of the practicalities involved, in terms of the food I ate, the clothes I wore, whether I should attend assembly, the practicalities of it at all. Once I overcame that there was the other thing, which was that they had very low expectations because they believed strongly that I couldn't speak very good English. I was born in Newcastle and I had a Geordie accent and the school I went to was in the south. They thought that the language problem was due to my not being able to speak English not just that I had a very strong regional accent. Consequently they forced me to have elocution lessons. They changed me. I lost the bit of character that I had and they moulded me into what they wanted me to be as opposed to what I wanted to be.' Neelam felt that the treatment she had was due to to the fact that she was Asian: 'in that environment, they were all girls, they were all blind and yet I was expected to have a lower IQ. I expect my Asian culture explained that.' Neelam talked about how she was socially isolated as well because of their assumptions about what she could and couldn't do: 'There were many many things, trips, discos that the teachers and the headmistress were very reluctant to let me attend mainly because I was Asian and they felt that my parents wouldn't approve. They hadn't asked what my parents were like, they hadn't judged what I was like, they judged the whole thing on my being Asian.'

Where teachers do not recognise racism or disablism, Black and ethnic minority children have little choice but to put up with bullying and persecution by other children. Sunita talked about how the children at her mainstream school used to call her 'Paki' and picked on her because she was deaf and Asian. 'I just had to ignore it; the teachers didn't help at all. I remember one day I complained after being called a "Paki" and the teacher said, "What's the matter with you, it's only a name."' Anita was bullied because she was both Asian and disabled. She talked of the 'teasing taunts from the other children in mainstream school calling me a "deaf Paki". I used to get called a lot of names because of the combination of being Black and being disabled.'

When Momta attended a segregated further education college, she felt the need to conform to the British way of life in order to be accepted: 'You had to learn to fit in. No vegetarian food was provided and I had to eat meat. If you didn't eat or mix, you were an outcast, literally. I had to dress like the others. You had to fit in. If you didn't conform, then you stood out a mile and you wouldn't be accepted.'

Momta also explained how going first to a mainstream school in Uganda and then to a segregated school in this country presented problems to her of acceptance of herself as a disabled person. Disabled people, too, pick up the stereotypes from society about themselves, as she explains: 'I thought, I don't belong here [in the special school], I don't want to be with these people. I am not like them. I picked up the perceptions that society has of us, it's in-built in us. That's the 'norm' that we are brought up with. As the only disabled child in a school of 300 or more people, you become, or try and think of yourself as one of the non-disabled people. And then you have to try and accept disability when you go into an environment where there are only disabled children. The system here is so unhealthy. It doesn't empower you.'

Shazia's impairment did not manifest itself until her teens and the main barrier she experienced was racism: 'The overlying memory I have of the education system is the racism actually because I was the only black girl in my class right the way through.' As a Muslim girl her parents did not want her to wear a school uniform, 'so I was different and set apart from the rest. There was a lot of bullying from other children and the teachers wouldn't do anything about it.'

To experience racism and disablism is to experience alienation and isolation, and the emotional consequences can be far-reaching. During both her primary and secondary school education Shazia was very isolated, as the only Black child and then as someone who they said had something 'wrong' with her. She decided in the end that she would 'prove them wrong in terms of my studies and achievements.' Shazia went through school very much keeping herself to herself and burying herself in books, because, by her teens, she was suffering from a double shock, 'one of isolation in an alien land and as the only black pupil in the top stream; and then as my disabilities started to appear from the pain and the shock of that.'

Shazia explained how the racist attitudes of teachers could get in the way of her educational progress. 'I had a white man for maths and he was absolutely racist. He sat there in a maths class and talked about his war experiences in Burma and in India and Africa. He would talk about how dirty Burmese, African and Indian people were. I was the only Black person there and he said all this in front of the class. He was really patronising and racist. It used to make me so mad that I would actually shake when I had a class with him and I actually started skipping school.'

In spite of experiences like this, Shazia felt that education was her salvation, 'I just hid myself in my books. Even though it was a way of escape it was also my salvation because through education, even though it was racist, through reading widely, I found that my route out. I felt that if I could do well that would give me choices and independence.'

Shazia's positive attitude towards her opportunities through education were not always shared by the white professionals with whom she came into contact. 'When I was at secondary school doing my O-Levels and the careers man asked me what I wanted to do, I said I wanted to go to university. He just looked at me and said "Oh, I wouldn't worry if I were you. In my experience whether you do your O-Levels or not most Asian girls are married off and having kids before you know it." He did not give me any advice about what he thought I should specialise in, or what he thought my capabilities were. He just looked at me with a smile on his face, as if to say, I don't know who you think you are kidding girl. I think that made me very angry and fearful at home because I kept thinking, is he right?'

A failure of mainstream further and higher education establishments to cater for disabled students can create a long-term frustration about missed opportunities. After leaving school Sunita went on to do a BTEC Diploma but she had to leave that before finishing the course because there was no sign language interpreter and she found it too much of a strain to lip read the teachers all the time. Sunita feels desperate at having missed out on her education and even though she is now married with three small children she is continuing to improve her education. She hopes to go to university after her children have grown up. 'I really want a good education, I really want to go to university, I really want it! want it! want it! But I can't because I have three small children, I have to do the housework and I have to feed my husband and I have to work to help my husband to pay the mortgage.'

Despite difficult experiences of education, some of the women interviewed retained the belief that achieving educational qualifications is the key to independence in adulthood. Their aspirations have been thwarted yet they remain ambitious for themselves. Anita's faith in the merits of a good education is strong and she has carried on studying part-time while working continuously for the past 10 years. 'My education was very poor and I resented this. I am very hot on education because it's the key to everything.' Anita hopes to become a teacher for deaf adults: 'I remember when I was a little girl my mum told me about being a teacher because she used to be a teacher in India. Because of that I wanted to be a teacher myself. And I was told "you can't be a teacher, you are deaf." I was so upset at this that for a long time I was ambitionless.'

While Jackie felt that her special school did not prepare her for life in any way, she has since struggled to make a better life for herself. She left school at the age of 16: 'I nearly had a nervous breakdown. When you left school you either went to college or took a horrible job that you didn't like because the job was for people with learning disabilities. So I went to college for four years. I did community care, home economics, return to study. I went to four different colleges during those four years. There was nothing else I could do. I couldn't sit at home like a zombie and watch television because the year after I left school I did that and it drove me crazy. So I had no choice but to motivate myself to keep my sanity. I had to fight, if I hadn't I wouldn't have been here today.'

It would seem that disabled Black and ethnic minority women experience a multiplicity of barriers – a combination of racism, sexism and disablism – in their pursuit for education. This will have major consequences for their labour market experiences where a good education is most critical.

Getting a job

At the point at which I interviewed them, nine of the women were in paid employment (two working part-time and seven full-time and two of these were self-employed). All had experienced difficulties in first entering the labour market on leaving school or higher education. Often, they related this to the inadequate preparation provided by their schooling. Neelam, for example, said that she felt that the segregated education she had did not prepare her in any way for the outside world: 'I was taught how to use opticon and various other bits of equipment, and mobility training, but I didn't have any experience of how to cope in the outside world, no life and social skills. I had no knowledge of how to deal with the outside world.'

The women's accounts of looking for paid employment are accounts of rejection and closed doors. Momta, who now works as a local government officer, explained that 'It took me two years of constant looking and applying and making telephone calls to get my first job. I did get quite a few interviews, but then when you actually turned up they didn't want anything to do with you. That was the biggest hurdle. Quite a lot of invitations for interviews were by phone so the employers didn't know anything about my disability at that stage. In those days application forms were very secondary, people just used to say "pop in for an interview". In some of the written applications I made, I did state my disability and yes I did get some interviews. But it is easy to say yes to someone on paper, the refusal usually came after the interviews.'

The Department of Employment provides Disablement Resettlement Officers (now called PACT – Placement, Assessment and Counselling Teams) whose role is to identify what help a disabled person needs to enter paid employment. Only three of the women interviewed, however, had contact with a DRO and their experiences were not positive ones. As Momta explained, 'I was very upset by her attitude. I didn't know what was available so I was in their hands and I was going to her and saying "Look I want to do something, you tell me what's available." "Well nothing, you haven't got any qualifications and how do you expect us to find you a job?" she said, "Nothing suitable is available." I can't remember all that she said but her facial expressions, her body language, the way she conducted herself with me was so disempowering, you know, you are belittled before you even begin. Those sorts of things you can't even put in words to explain.'

Momta finally got her first job after constant badgering of another DRO to try to help her to get an interview. 'There was one vacancy which looked possible – a clerical and administrative worker at a health service – and she had spoken to the secretary there. 'I had an interview with a man from the health service unit, and I impressed him. I got my first job and I was there for about six and a half years.'

Neelam, too, sought help from a DRO, but felt that it was assumed that, as a visually impaired woman, the only job opportunity open to her was to be a telephonist or typist. She also found that the DRO asked questions about her dress, her living with her family and whether she would be able to cope with working with men. 'She felt that living with my family would compromise my independence and that I was incapable because I was living with my family. It didn't occur to her that this was for economic reasons; I couldn't afford my own place. She felt that I was inadequate. I generally wore skirts and tops and she thought that I was being false and that I normally wore Asian clothes. She couldn't accept that that was the way I dressed. She thought I couldn't handle working with men.'

A number of the women found that they could only attain low-skilled, low-paid work. Anita, for example, could initially only get work 'in a factory doing very monotonous work which involved putting caps on the fuses that you put inside plugs. I was one of the fastest there but it was so monotonous I felt that it was not meant for me and that I was capable of doing more.' She left this job and went to college evening classes to do O-levels with the hope of getting an office job. Eventually Anita got a job as a clerical assistant in the civil service. She carried on with her education part-time and she is now a social worker. Few of the women interviewed received much help from the employment service or from other professionals to overcome the disadvantages of an inadequate education or the discriminatory attitudes of employers.

Laila found that her only option after five years of un-successful job seeking was to become self-employed. 'For about five years it was a low period because no matter what direction I tried I was met with rejection after rejection. I finally realised that no matter how qualified I was I would not be accepted. So I decided to go into voluntary work which I did for about seven years before becoming self-employed. I was terrified of cutting the cord with the benefit system because you become so dependent on it.'

Neelam made over 100 applications before she got one

interview. She stated both her impairment and her ethnic origin on all the application forms but believes that it was disability that most affected her chances. 'There wasn't an application form for the first job I went for. My family had seen it advertised in the paper. It was to do tele working: selling stuff over the telephone. I rang up and I sold myself brilliantly. I was nearly offered the job. They said, "Yes, why don't you come along?" And then I thought I'd better be honest, I'd better tell them about my disability. There was an immediately cold voice on the end of a telephone. They said, "I am afraid we don't think you will be able to do the job, terribly sorry, we are looking for somebody else. We will call you back, we will keep you on record." Thank you, but no thank you, it was basically.'

It seems to be quite common that employers make assumptions about a disabled person's inability to do certain things which are considered to be essential for a particular post. Neelam described how 'When I was looking for my second job and sending off millions of applications, I actually received a letter back from one of the local papers, clearly stating, "I am sorry we can't offer you the job as we don't think you are capable because you are blind."' The job was to sell advertising space which, by then, Neelam had experience of doing. 'So I knew how to work around it, I knew how to deal with sizes, how to deal with spacing on a particular brochure, how to know how many inches it was, how to sell that across to somebody, and how to make sure their advert looked the best on the paper, I knew all of that, I knew how to work myself around it. But they didn't question that, they just knew that I couldn't see and that I couldn't do the job. It didn't occur to them that there would be ways around it.'

Laila said 'I never got as far as interviews because I had to ask if buildings were accessible, and their attitude changed as soon as I asked about access.' She recounted one telephone conversation with a prospective employer who, once Laila stated that she used a wheelchair, said, '"Oh well, in that case it would be a waste of your time and mine." I asked, "Why?" she said, "Because you would be expected to make tea, there are four people in the office." I said, "I am quite capable of making tea, I make tea for myself". She said, "No, I am telling you now it would be a waste of your time and mine, goodbye," and put the phone down. That was the most obvious one, others were a bit more subtle, like I would phone up and they would say "Yes, we will let you know when the interview is", and when I phoned up again and they would say, "We have given the job to somebody else".'

Mary, who is blind, experienced direct discrimination while looking for a job as a typist with one of the leading tabloid newspapers: 'I had a test which was pathetically easy, English test, typing and shorthand, I passed everything. The head of the typing department said, "I will employ you no problem". I thought I had a job there, then when we rang up to see what word processors they use and all that, to assess my equipment needs, they said, "Oh, we haven't definitely offered her a job", and they started saying, "We would like to employ you but so and so was wondering who is going to check your work." I was absolutely disgusted because I had passed all their tests with flying colours and at the time they were really enthusiastic but then they had second thoughts about employing a disabled person. I think the woman herself was quite genuine but the people above her said no.'

Another paper Mary applied to said, '"Oh, we are really concerned that the girls would spoil you and somebody would have to check your work." They were just looking for excuses not to employ me.'

A number of the women felt they were put at a particular disadvantage because of the lack of anti-discrimination legislation concerning disabled people. Neelam, for example, felt that because there is no legislation to prohibit discrimination against disabled people, employers feel able to overtly express their discriminatory attitudes. 'I think if you are an ethnic minority or if you are a woman, there is protection, but there isn't that protection, there is no legislation, for disabled people.'

Apart from the attitude of employers, there are a number of physical barriers which confronted the women interviewed. For those with mobility impairments, the first barrier is that of getting into the place of interview as Momta explained: 'It was quite difficult with some places. I couldn't get in, even when they said I could. And then you get there and there are a couple of steps and then another step and so on and you have to rely on other people to get you in and you think, forget it, this isn't going to work.' Jo, who is a trained teacher and uses callipers, found that the physical inaccessibility of most schools was a big barrier to her getting a job. 'Nine out of 10 schools are inaccessible for disabled people.' Even at schools that were reasonably accessible Jo found herself questioning her ability to cope. 'I was basically failing the interviews. They would always have a tour around the school and I would always feel disheartened because even when a place was physically okay, in that the classroom was accessible, I would always be lagging behind. The tour was designed so that you could meet people and ask questions. The other candidates would pointedly wait, but I would still miss out on vital conversation and feel out of it. So by the time I got to the interview itself, I would be out of it and feeling that it wouldn't work physically anyway. I would compare myself with other candidates and think myself at a disadvantage because they would be able to do extra curricular activities such as after-school tennis.'

For visually impaired women such as Neelam, there are barriers right at the beginning of the process of job seeking: 'Information is all in print, adverts are in print, the applications are always in print, I never had access to such information.' And then, as she explained, after overcoming these access and attitudinal barriers and getting to the interview against all the odds, 'there is the whole thing of having to prove that you can do the job. You had to say, I have this and that and the other equipment, I can do it. If you didn't have that backing, if you didn't have the knowledge that you could gain the equipment, there is no way you could have done the job, they just wouldn't accept you.'

Those who are successful at getting a job have to develop strategies for dealing with employers' prejudices. Jo eventually managed to get part-time teaching posts which gave her confidence in herself, and was then able to obtain a full-time teaching position. She quickly demonstrated her abilities as a good teacher which brought a promotion to head of business studies. However, due to worries about the security of some expensive computer equipment, her office was moved to the second floor where she became isolated as a result of being unable to keep going up and down the stairs to the staff room. Jo then moved on to work as a sales person with a recruitment agency. Again she found access to be a major problem as this time her office was on the fourth floor and even though there was a lift 'it kept breaking down and it was a nightmare. The company's attitude was, how you cope is up to you.' As a result Jo has made a conscious decision to stop working for others and to become self-employed.

Jo has had to rely on assertiveness and her own confidence in herself to overcome both physical and attitudinal barriers. Such self-confidence, however, may be hard to attain when the experience of schooling and entering the labour market is such a negative one.

Conclusion

There are many facets to the discrimination that disabled Black and ethnic minority women experience. I hope that this chapter will provide a starting point for other disabled Black and ethnic minority women to make their experiences known.

Disabled Black and ethnic minority women experience a multiplicity of barriers resulting from the combination of disablism, racism and sexism. As Anita explains 'it happens singularly, plurally and multiply, and it's the totality that counts at the end of the day. You are thought of as completely inferior because you are all three things.'

The fact that these impact upon the quality of education and the type of employment to which we have access, dictates the overall quality of our daily lives. However, it is also clear that these women possess an indomitable spirit and overwhelming determination to succeed in the face of a multitude of negative attitudes from peers, teachers, prospective employers and, in some cases, their own families.

We can take heart from our determination to rise above our oppressive situations, and while we continue to be so resilient, discrimination and oppression in its many guises will not have a free reign in our lives.

CHAPTER THREE

ENCOUNTERS WITH STRANGERS:
The public's responses to disabled women and how this affects our sense of self
Lois Keith

The first time I went out in my wheelchair without another adult I was going just around the corner to see an accessible flat which I was hoping to rent. I had been in hospital for five months, home but always accompanied for the next two or three and this was an important, confidence-building trip for me. I was taking control of my life again. I wasn't completely alone, my four-year-old daughter was with me and this was another important feature of this journey: we were out on our own together, mother and daughter.

As we neared our first corner, a man I had never seen before, far from young and definitely wobbly on his pins, stopped straight ahead of me and said. 'Are you all right love, shall I give you a push?' Now this might have been laughable if it wasn't so intrusive. Of the two of us, I was definitely the most mobile even as a neophyte wheelchair user. However, I hadn't yet developed the antennae which would help me to predict what was going to happen next and I was just trying to work out how I should respond when he lurched at me, taking hold of the back of my wheelchair, nearly knocking it and me off balance. I was so surprised I didn't know what to do and mumbling something pathetic like, 'I'm fine really, please let go,' and I just kind of pushed harder round the corner, while my daughter said 'why did he do that mummy, do we know him?'

This probably wasn't the first of what I have come to call 'Encounters with Strangers', a term I owe partly to Robert Murphy and his book *The Body Silent*, but it is the first I remember, because it brought home so forcibly the difference between how I wanted to see myself, as a now visibly different but still a competent and private person and how others saw me and would continue to see me.

As Robert Murphy says, 'The recently disabled person faces the world with a changed body and an altered identity – which even by itself would make his(sic) re-entry into society a delicate and chancy matter. But his future is made even more perilous by the way he is treated by the non-disabled, including some of his oldest friends and associates and even family members.' (Murphy, 1987, p. 96).

Disabled people have to work continually against destructive forces which see us as powerless, passive and unattractive. It seems that no matter how cheerfully and positively we attempt to go out into the world, we are bound to be confronted by someone whose response to our lack of ordinariness, our difference from the norm leaves us feeling powerless and angry. Trying to understand the complicated feelings which arise out of our everyday encounters with the world is central to the lives of all disabled people.

In fact, if you bring any group of disabled people together, before too long we'll be swapping stories about the annoying, appalling, patronising, insensitive, unhelpful and sometimes just plain funny encounters that we have on an almost daily basis with shop assistants, taxi drivers, people standing next to us in queues, lifts or waiting rooms, the doctor, the doctor's receptionist, people in restaurants and cinemas, people who come to service our washing machines or cars or just plain anybody who passes us in the street.

This isn't because disabled people are incapable of ordinary social intercourse. Indeed we have a whole set of rather sophisticated techniques for dealing with people we hardly know or are unlikely to meet again. It is because these encounters and the questions, comments and stares which accompany them, although they are rarely overtly hostile, are almost always unsettling and intrusive, forcing us all the time to realise how hard it is to go about the ordinary business of life in our unordinary physical bodies.

Doing disability all day long can be an exhausting process. I don't mean having an impairment, in my own case not being able to walk. Like most disabled people I can deal with this. I mean having to spend a significant part of each day dealing with a physical world which is historically designed to exclude me and, even more tiring, dealing with other people's pre-conceptions and misconceptions about me. If disabled people are to come out of these encounters confident and whole, we have to understand what is going on. We have to learn to channel these experiences, filter them and make sense of them – holding on to our pride and our right to go about our daily business in our own independent and private way.

I 'do disability' all day long, because the fact is that in my everyday encounters with the world, the first thing others look at is my wheelchair and this colours and informs how they see me. This isn't always obvious and it isn't always awful – frequently people are genuine in their desire to be friendly and helpful. But even their smiles affirm my status in their eyes as someone they are glad they are not. The assumptions about what using a wheelchair means (their language is 'confined to a wheelchair' and 'wheelchair bound') is so overwhelmingly negative and so very different to how I want to see myself, that unless I have ways of understanding and dealing with these encounters, they have the power to destroy me.

Being defined by others in a way you don't choose to define yourself is not, of course, a problem exclusive to disabled people. Women have for many years been writing about our need to reject being defined exclusively by our bodies and the way we look, but it is different for disabled people because some of us deviate so significantly from what is considered to be within the range of 'normal' appearance. Of course, not all disabled people use wheelchairs and not all disabled people are women, but I will focus mostly on this particular group of disabled people, not only because this is the group I know best, but also because the wheelchair has come to be seen as a symbol of need and dependency and people bring a whole set of assumptions into the encounters they have with those of us who use them for our mobility. Many of the comments and observations about the experiences of wheelchair users will, however, be all too familiar to a lot of other disabled people and to all those who are obviously physically 'different'.

All social encounters are governed by rules of behaviour. There are things that it is normally acceptable for strangers to say to each other and things that are not. For example, in the particular section of British society in which I usually mix, it is considered okay, indeed complimentary, to remark that people are thin, but rude to say that they are fat. It is acceptable to tell people that they are very tall but impolite to remark on the fact that they are unusually short. And there are things that people feel they can say to disabled people which they wouldn't dream of saying to anyone else.

Erving Goffman has written that the very starting point and core of all social interaction is the establishment by the people involved of stances of what he calls 'deference and demeanour'. Each party must comport herself or himself as a person of worth and substance, and each must put social space and distance around the self. The other, in turn, respects this demeanour by according it deference (Goffman, 1956). Robert Murphy, commenting on this work, goes on to describe how,

> The extent of this mutual respect varies of course with the situation and the people involved, and the way in which it is expressed is an artefact of culture. It occurs through a subconscious grammar of gesture and verbal nuance, a language so subtle that it escapes the awareness of both parties, except when it is withheld or altered – as it so often is in encounters with people who are physically impaired. (Murphy, 1987, p. 102)

The best example I know of this is a recent story told to me by a close friend. This friend, a woman in her early forties, was recently returning to London by Inter-City train after a high-level meeting at a Government Department. She was smartly dressed and carried her lap-top computer. She had returned on the early evening train and was waiting at the taxi rank with all the other men and women returning from their day's work. However, the taxi driver did not see a business woman returning home from work. What he saw was the wheelchair. As soon as my friend was seated in his cab, he said, 'Been handicapped long, love?' Busy with thoughts of the meeting and what she was going to have for supper, she replied evasively, 'Yes, for some time.' Undeterred, the driver went on, 'Get very depressed do you?' 'What depresses me,' my friend said, glad for once that she had found the right answer at the right time, 'is people asking me personal questions they don't have any right to ask!'

To be fair, the driver realised he had overstepped the mark and apologised immediately with 'That's a fair point. Sorry.' And the rest of the short journey through London was conducted in silence. But the point is of course not that the driver had been rude but that he had read the wheelchair as the sole indicator of how he should behave. The other signals which he might normally use: dress, time and place of arrival, age, manner of speaking, were insignificant compared to the fact that he was giving a ride to a 'handicapped person'. Of course gender issues are relevant here and to some extent he was using the language and behaviour men often use towards women. But the most important factor in this encounter is that like many people faced with an unknown person in a wheelchair, he saw a damaged exterior and therefore felt free to ignore the normal social conventions which tell us we must be silent about what we see as negative attributes in others. He asked questions which assumed that the quality of her life was poor and depressing and she was denied respect. After all, this driver must have had many 40-something businessmen in his cab but you can't imagine him asking them, 'Been bald long, have you mate? Get depressed about it?'

As Robert Murphy says, 'A serious disability [i.e. impairment] inundates all other claims to social standing, relegating to secondary status all attainments of life, all other social roles, even sexuality. It is not a role, it is an identity, a dominant characteristic to which all social roles must be adjusted' (Murphy, 1987, p. 90).

For many years, Goffman's work on stigma provided the most helpful account of what happened to disabled people in such social encounters as the one described above. He argued that society categorised people, and that there are a number of attributes you need to be classed as ordinary and natural in each group. When a stranger comes in front of us and is seen as possessing a characteristic which makes them different to others in that category, an attribute or feature which is less desirable, that person is reduced in our minds 'from a whole and usual person, to a tainted, discounted one'. Such an attribute, Goffman called a stigma but it may also be called a failing or a handicap (Goffman, 1963, p. 12).

Where someone has a very visible difference such as using a wheelchair, the rules of behaviour are not clear and all kinds of confusions and problems arise. As Murphy says,

> The disabled person must make an extra effort to establish his status as an autonomous, worthy individual but the reaction of the other party may totally undercut these pretensions through some thoughtless act or omission. Even if the able bodied person is making a conscious attempt to pay deference to the disabled party, he must struggle against the underlying ambiguity of the encounter, the lack of clear cultural guidelines on how to behave and perhaps his own sense of revulsion. (Murphy, 1987, p. 103)

This lack of cultural guidelines, means that social situations between the two parties make for anxious, unanchored interaction. All sorts of rules, including the rules of polite behaviour become altered and distorted and strangers feel that they can approach the 'stigmatised individual' as long as they appear to be 'sympathetic to their plight'. (Goffman, 1963, p. 28).

Goffman's work has been justifiably criticised by many writers who object to the way the blame seems to fall on the 'stigmatised person' for being in possession of these unwanted 'attributes'. His language, too, is often offensive, he describes disabled people as falling into the category of 'the abominations of the body, the various physical deformities' (p. 14). His work is also criticised by writers who want to take our understanding of the power relationships in society beyond merely describing what happens in individual encounters between disabled and non-disabled people. Michael Oliver argues in his book, *The Politics of Disablement*, that we need to 'throw off the shackles of the individualistic approach to disability with its focus on the discredited and the discreditable and to give an account of the collective experiences of disabled people in terms of the structural notions of discrimination and oppression.' (Oliver, 1990, p. 68).

However, whilst Goffman's analysis of the encounters between two parties where one is visibly different, failed to understand the structural sources and roots of the prejudices and seemed to blame the disabled person for being 'deficient', he was correct in realising that it is important to understand what is happening in these encounters. A detailed examination of what is meant by the smiles, the patronising gestures, the questions, the stares, the rudeness and the rejection should not just be dismissed as the stuff of apolitical individualism or relegated to psychological studies. An analysis of these apparently minor, but actually very significant events in the lives of disabled people, what they mean and what effects they have on us, is part of the political progress disabled people are making. In her book, *Pride Against Prejudice*, Jenny Morris argues that we must find ways to avoid internalising *their* values into *our* lives. 'One of the biggest problems for disabled people is that all these undermining messages, which we receive every day of our lives from the non-disabled world which surrounds us, become part of our way of thinking about ourselves' (Morris, 1991, p. 22).

In order to avoid letting their ideas of us into our heads, we must first understand what is going on. People may feel that they are being, to use Goffman's words, 'sympathetic to the plight of persons of our kind' but the fact is that we don't see it like this. Their smiles, questions and comments reinforce the feeling that whatever image we might have of ourselves, society imposes a negative identity upon us and much of our social life is a struggle against this. Strangers do not let us forget that their perception of us is dominated by the ways in which we are different.

People like myself, who rely upon their wheelchair for mobility and independence, see it as a piece of liberating

equipment. I have a certain fondness towards my own little
black number and feel anxious whenever it is out of my reach,
panicky if it is out of my sight. I don't always like the sight of
myself in it – what woman would when we live in a society
whose idea of female beauty is the slim, taut, well-muscled
body, dressed in skin tight skirts with stiletto heels? But I like
myself well enough and enjoy wearing clothes, shoes and the
odd bit of adornment to suit my present shape and needs.

However, it is a distinctly minority view to see the wheelchair as an object of liberation. For most people it symbolises a
vast range of negative attributes which include dependence,
need, infirmity of mind and body, sickness, and a curious
combination of the qualities which are seen to pertain to both
childhood and old age. This can be illustrated by the kind of
questions people routinely ask people in wheelchairs. In a
recent discussion I had with a group of friends when I was
preparing to write this piece, we drew up a list of questions
that complete strangers had asked us over the past few weeks.
These included:

 - What did you do to yourself then? (this has many
   variations, the most common of which is, 'what happened to
   you?')
 - Do you live with your parents?
 - Why do you use that kind of wheelchair?
 - What are you going to do when you want to go to the
   toilet? (on an aeroplane)
 - Is anyone meeting you? (on a train)
 - Do you get depressed a lot?
 - Have you got your brakes on? (at the theatre)
 - Does it hurt?
 - Have you passed your driving test? (also expressed as 'do
   you need a license for that?' This one is supposed to be a
   joke.)
 - Can you walk at all?
 - Are you going to get better?

It may be possible to dismiss these questions as annoying but
relatively meaningless intrusions on our privacy, but this

would be to ignore what is behind them. What people really think when they see someone in a wheelchair (unless we can assure them that it's only temporary and that soon we will be up and running about) is that this must be an unbearable condition for us, one which they would do anything to avoid.

It is not uncommon for people to suggest that having to use a wheelchair must be a fate worse than death. I came across something to that effect three times in one day. The first was an article in the *Guardian* newspaper about a woman who had had silicone breast implants after a mastectomy. These ruptured and she became seriously ill. She said, 'soon afterwards my hip began hurting and it became so bad that I had to use a wheelchair. I've fought my way out of that now and stagger around on crutches because I'm damned if I'm going to submit to a wheelchair at my age.' The second was a radio play I listened to in the afternoon about a father of a young boy born with a physical impairment which affected his mobility. The father was determined that his son would learn to walk, relentlessly training him to run a mile, and the play ended with his triumphant statement, 'I've sent it back to the hospital, we don't have to have that damned wheelchair in the house any more.' The third was a story told to me by a woman I had gone to see about altering a jacket for me. Her mother, who had a disease of the nervous system remained house-bound for the last two years of her life, refusing to go out because she could not bear to see herself, or be seen, in a wheelchair.

The wheelchair is the symbol of dependence. As one woman said to me, people read it as a badge which says 'I need help'. For her this was positive. She has an adult son who has acute communication and learning difficulties. He is able to walk but has no concentration and is very unco-ordinated. When they are struggling together, people feel awkward and embarrassed and turn away but when he is in a wheelchair they rush to open doors and help them up kerbs or steps. People are glad to help in this case because they feel that they know what to do, the rules of behaviour are clear to them. Where they are less clear is when wheelchair users challenge their expectations by refusing to accept their assistance and patronage.

Although disabled people come in all shapes and sizes and

there are an enormous range of impairments and degrees of impairment, some of which are obvious to outsiders, some invisible, it is the wheelchair that is *the* symbolic representation of disability and impairment. The wheelchair logo is the symbol you see on lavatory doors, in parking places, by ramped entrances and at supermarket checkouts and is supposed to include *all* disabled people. (This is a matter of understandable annoyance to those who have quite different requirements for assistance.) The average person feels that they know about wheelchairs. If you asked people to do one of those surveys where they had to come up with quick word associations with 'wheelchair', I expect that the list would be something like: 'elderly, sick, dependent, help, need, confined, bound'. Pushed for details you might get: 'sad, lonely, brave, courageous', or even, 'tartan blanket and furry slippers'.

However, the significance society attaches to wheelchairs and those who use them (in that order) is never simple. At the same time as the wheelchair is an artefact that most people associate with illness and old age, it is also a wheeled chair, which is not very far from a push chair, the cultural significance of which is babyhood and childishness. This should not surprise us as the states of babyhood and old age are already linked in our minds. In *As You Like It*, Shakespeare's character Jaques reminds us that the seventh stage of man is just a 'second childishness and mere oblivion, sans teeth, sans eyes, sans everything'.

Everyone else is taller than us, we go about in wheeled chairs, sometimes we need to be pushed – we must be babies. Everyone who uses a wheelchair can tell you stories about asking a question and having the reply addressed to the person you are with or people coming behind you and pushing you, even being patted on the head. I have a number of stories of my own about encounters where people seemed to associate me with the state of babyhood. On one occasion I was with my children trying to get into a wonderful experience of colour and music called 'Colourspace' held in a large open space at The Barbican in London. When I asked the ticket seller if this was accessible to wheelchair users she replied innocently 'Oh no, I don't think so because we don't allow baby-buggies in there.' She was amazed at my anger, unwilling to listen to me telling her that this was not the same thing at all and that I was the mother here, responsible for my children.

A friend of mine tells another story, which also took place in a large arts complex, of trying to take his son and daughter into the Children's Film Club on a Saturday morning. Although this cinema is accessible for wheelchair users, he was told that they would not allow him to take his children inside because 'you don't have an adult with you.'

Just as in our society babies are not quite considered to be 'whole' people, especially in public places (where the very English view that children should be seen and not heard predominates), people in wheelchairs are considered to be not quite whole either. We are expected to be kind to babies and children but not to grant them exactly the same rights as adults at a stage in their lives when they wouldn't know how to handle them. We do expect them to grow into autonomous and independent adults capable of taking responsibility for those younger than them. This is not the case with disabled people.

The cultural message that you must be kind to 'the handicapped', is a very powerful one. It acts as a mechanism which both distances the 'giver' of kindness from the recipient and allows them permission to patronise. The idea of caring for and caring about people who are less fortunate than ourselves is important even in the current non-religious, materialistic climate of our society, but unfortunately this state of goodwill and generosity often works to disempower disabled people. The other day on BBC Radio 4, I heard a restaurant owner expressing the view that the Civil Rights Bill for Disabled People would put him out of business if it was ever passed and that he could not afford to make the changes he thought were required. 'Please don't get me wrong', he whined, 'I've got nothing against disability people, I love disability people. I give a lot of money to charity.' The more disabled people stayed away from his restaurant, the more he liked them. Giving money to charity was his way of making sure things stayed that way.

The role of Charity, both in terms of giving money to large

organisations who 'look after' disabled people and in terms of being kind and nice to those less fortunate than ourselves is at the root of the relationship between disabled and non-disabled people in both political and individual situations. Charities create a culture of dependency and we are expected to feel grateful for what we are given. As Jenny Morris argues, 'Our gratitude is an essential part of the relationship; charity is actually about making the non-disabled person feel good about themselves. Our gratitude is the gift we are expected to make in exchange for tolerance and material help' (Morris, 1991, p. 108).

What harm is there in being grateful for the help that others give you? Well, none if that help is freely offered on equal terms with nothing required in return except a simple 'Thankyou'. All the wheelchair users I know say an awful lot of thankyou's each day and we do so quite happily when people open heavy doors for us, see us sitting looking at a steep ramp and ask us if we'd like a push, offer to take a tray full of cups of tea to the nearest table for us, remove a chair so we can sit at the table and drink it or make any of the other thoughtful gestures which many people do each day. This is non-threatening, non-invasive assistance which makes both parties feel good about the other. It works on the basis that people will stop and look at us, ask if we would like a hand and move on if we say no.

The problems come when people's motives for offering help are not so straightforward. When their offer to 'help' you is based on their need, not yours. This is brilliantly told in Janice's Pink's poem 'Do Unto Others' which tells the (true) story of her encounter with a woman at a supermarket checkout. This woman, alerting the cashier's attention to the fact that 'we've got a cripple here', proceeds to grab Janice's bag, declaring that it is 'the least that I can do/because but for the grace of God, I could be just like you!' But her 'thoughtfulness' soon turns to outrage when Janice begins to make it clear that she finds this behaviour both interfering and offensive. The poem ends with the lecture the do-gooder felt she needed to give to the ungrateful Janice.

I know you're being very brave, but that *was* rather rude –
Next time someone helps you, try to show some gratitude.
Of course you think life isn't fair, but when you're feeling
  blue –
Big smile! And then remember, there's someone worse than
  you!' (Pink, 1994)

We are not supposed to understand that non-disabled people
feel uncomfortable at our presence in the world and that what
they sometimes feel is more than discomfort, it is revulsion.
The central confusion of the relationship between us is that on
the one hand they are disconcerted by our presence, and are
confused about how to behave towards us or even what words
they should use to describe us, but on the other hand they
have a clear idea that they should be helpful and kind. Our part
of the bargain is to ignore their unease and confusion and
accept the 'help'. Our gratefulness is part of the lie that
everything is really alright between us.

We are certainly not supposed to get angry. We are expected
to remain silent when they park in the spot reserved for
disabled drivers ('there's no need to use that tone of voice to
me, there just wasn't anywhere else to park' or even 'Well, I
don't fucking care'). We're not supposed to tell them that we
will not accept their rule that we can't come and see the film in
this cinema because people in wheelchairs pose a health and
safety hazard ('Don't shout at me dear, I'm only doing my job').
We are supposed to laugh at their remarks about how much
room we take up, what a problem we are getting through
doors, whether we have a licence to drive a dangerous vehicle
('Can't you take a joke dear?' or 'I can see you've got a chip on
your shoulder'). We are expected to tolerate their stares and if
we dare to challenge them they say 'I was only looking to see if
you needed any help'.

I never enjoy these kind of confrontations and work hard to
avoid them. Like most women, I do a lot of smiling and saying
'thankyou' and 'sorry'. But sometimes I come up against a
situation which brings me face to face with the hostility which
often lies not far beneath the veneer of kindness and concern.
However often this happens, it always surprises me and it

always hurts. As Nancy Mairs says, it usually occurs when 'I stop being a jolly cripple, a Tiny Tim peering over the edge of the Christmas table, waving my crutch and piping down God's blessing on everyone and turn instead into Caliban, a most scurvy monster' (Mairs, 1988). It happens in situations where I tell people, even when I tell them politely, what I really feel.

I have written about one of these occasions in a piece called 'This Week I've Been Rushed Off My Wheels'. It happened in a narrow street in London after I had been out for a meal with a friend:

> I was getting into my car when the all-too-familiar happened. In a busy road, with cars parked on both sides, I kept the traffic waiting whilst I folded my wheelchair into the nifty mechanical hoist which stacks it on the roof of my car. A thirty-something, City banker, BMW type approached offering much-unneeded help, and tried to close the door, which clearly wouldn't shut what with the hoist very slowly moving its way up.
>
> I was pleased with the way I dealt with this one, uttering a pithy phrase like 'Leave my door alone, you stupid idiot, can't you see you'll just have to wait' and at the exact moment, slamming the door shut. Furious, his face now scarlet, he swore at me through the closed window, insisting he was only trying to be helpful. (Keith, 1994)

The friend I was with, as well as many non-disabled people who have read this piece have been upset by my reaction which they felt was unnecessarily aggressive. Wasn't he just trying to be helpful? Would they have their heads similarly bitten off if they offered help to a disabled person? But I felt that he wasn't being helpful. There was nothing he could do to speed things up, he was just being impatient. I didn't want him holding on to my car door, making me feel bad about keeping the traffic waiting, regarding me as someone dependent on his help. I felt angry and I showed it. People find this anger hard to cope with. I find it hard myself.

However, I should have felt good about this incident. I had understood the superficiality of his concern and dealt with it appropriately which in this case was angrily. But women, particularly, find it hard to know how to handle all the anger that such chance encounters with strangers can bring. They always have the potential to damage our fragile sense of ourselves as independent, private people. This is why it is so important to interpret what is going on and to recognise the gestures and questions which may seem to others as concern for our welfare, or curiosity about the conditions of our lives, but are experienced by us as unfriendly, invasive and patronising.

This is why it is so important for disabled people to get together, to talk, to write and to listen to what others have to say. The disabled people's movement and the growing disabled people's culture reognise our need to examine our common heritage and shared experiences and the ways in which these oppress us. Trying to understand what is going on in these encounters, analysing our reactions, is not just an act of self preservation, it is also important in understanding the power relationships which exist in the relationships between disabled and non-disabled people. As Jenny Morris says,

> The manifestations of prejudice are often not out in the open; they are the hidden assumptions about us which form the bedrock of most of our interactions with the non-disabled world. It is often difficult for us to identify *why* someone's behaviour makes us so angry, or feel undermined. Our anger and insecurity can thus seem unreasonable not just to others but also, sometimes, to ourselves. (Morris, 1991, p. 18)

Unfortunately, the world doesn't really seem to like disabled people taking strength from being together, at least not in public. The common view of being kind and charitable to us is that the public is willing to tolerate us one at a time but feels deeply uncomfortable when there are too many of us together.

I once had the misfortune to try to eat in a popular, award-winning fish and chip shop in North London. I had rung to ask whether it was accessible and they had advised me to get there early which I did. What I hadn't said was that there would be *two* of us in wheelchairs, with one other adult and our three young children.

Right from the start their manner was unwelcoming to the point of hostility. They told my children to say 'thank you' to the couple who offered them seats at their table because they were just leaving. They hustled us all into a corner but said that we couldn't move two tables together because the waitress wouldn't be able to get round them, (this wasn't true) then they ignored us. Eventually we left, all of us angry and upset, me to the point of tears. What was clear from their behaviour was that whilst the presence of one wheelchair user could be seen as benevolent patronage, two of us lowered the tone. We were far too depressing an image for this relentlessly trendy, salt-of-the-earth restaurant.

Disabled people often feel undermined by such perceptions of us as less attractive, undesirable, and as objects of concern or pity. For women, our sense of ourselves is formed, developed and indeed damaged by how others see us. We learn early on in our lives to define ourselves through our attachments and relationships with others. In her book, *In a Different Voice*, Carol Gilligan writes about how relationships, and particularly issues of dependence, are experienced differently by men and women. From their childhood, boys and men learn to see themselves as separate and independent individuals whilst girls and women are much more inclined to define themselves through their relationships and attachments (Gilligan, 1982, Chapter 1).

In our dealings with a disabling world, whilst both disabled men and disabled women struggle with the balance between dependence and independence, it is likely that women care more about needing to please others, wanting to be helpful, to make everything alright.

Michele Wates, a woman who in the following quote is still walking although with great difficulty, describes an encounter with someone she doesn't know and will never meet again. She is collecting her children from school.

Seeing the averted gaze of pity, she found herself preparing for the moment when they would pass one another on the narrow path. She could not help herself from wanting people, even complete strangers like this man, to notice that although she might be dragging herself along like a wounded animal, her eyes were bright, she had a ready smile and her voice, if he should have reason to hear it, was up and out; confident.

Increasingly, she asked herself why it should be necessary to put so much effort into convincing people that she was in good shape psychically, if not physically. (Wates, 1994)

I imagine that Michele's struggle was against the new, unwelcome identity that had been imposed on her and which she experienced through the looks, the gestures and the questions of others. Like all disabled people whose bodies contravene the values of youth, beauty, health and freedom, she had to struggle against being seen by others and therefore seeing herself, as not just someone with a flawed body, but as an inadequate person. Like many women, Michele felt that with her bright smile and sparkling eyes, it was her responsibility to make everything alright. But our desire to make everything easier for ourselves by always being bright and pleasant in our dealings with the world and our need to have everyone think well of us, can be destructive.

If we go about our business in this way, it means that we are always putting ourselves in the position of being passive and grateful and are denying our justified anger and rage. We have to learn ways to resist the power of these encounters to belittle us but not in a way which leaves us feeling appalled at our own behaviour. Women have been conditioned to say sorry for things that are not their fault, in order to make the other person feel better. And sometimes women in wheelchairs can pose some difficulties for others. We do take up a lot of space, sometimes we run over people's toes or need others to move something out of the way for us, so that we can go about our business. But it is important that we do not keep apologising for our very existence.

Anger is another difficulty for those of us brought up to think our role in life is to smooth over the cracks, to make everyone feel all right. I hardly ever feel better for really losing my temper in encounters with the world, even when I am certain that my anger is justified. Most women just aren't programmed like that. Instead, like most of the disabled people I know, I have worked hard at building up a range of techniques of resistance to those encounters which force us to respond.

One of these techniques is avoidance, often through pretending ignorance. People are often confused by this but not too surprised since they half assume we're not in full possession of our reasoning powers. An example of this occured when I was shopping with my daughters a couple of weeks ago. The assistant, assuming familiarity because I had opened up a conversation with her, (I'd asked if they stocked jeans with elasticated waists) suddenly said 'What did you do to yourself then?' I was momentarily taken aback but dealt with it by answering a completely different question to the one she had asked. With the good manners my mother had taught me, I replied, 'Well, I'm out with my daughters, I'm buying some clothes for them to start the new term.' This response had the desired effect of silencing her, but disconcerted us all.

Another tactic for dealing with undermining questions and responses is to take on the role of educator. You explain to them why you think they are behaving inappropriately, how it makes you feel and what they need to do to alter their attitude. This is worthwhile but exhausting and should only be done when the stranger is going to become a colleague or a neighbour or someone you have to have some sort of relationship with. Sometimes I find myself doing it anyway, like the first time someone said to my children, who were then only aged four and six, 'Are you good girls who always look after mummy?' I was so upset and angry at this that I couldn't help myself saying that, no, they didn't look after me, they were little children. I looked after them, and she really shouldn't assume that because I was disabled I was incapable of being a parent. I don't know what good it did her, but it was important to say it if only to help my daughters understand what was going on here and for them to know that there were ways of resisting it.

Sarcasm, swearing or shouting are possibilities but I try to refrain from these responses because like most women, I feel uncomfortable with open agression. I'd like to be able to offer the perfect one-liner but this doesn't come easily. I did think of one once when I was struggling with a heavy lavatory door and a woman came up to me and said 'I used to be a nurse, would you like some help?' and I replied, 'No thank you, I need a pee, not an injection.'

Another possibility is to anticipate the difficulties and get in first. I have quite a good technique for this which helps me over the painful business of confirming a stranger's view of myself as a helpless creature. In situations where I need assistance in getting up a kerb or a steep ramp, I wait until I see a suitable person and ask them, 'Would you like to do your good deed for the day?' This subtly alters the power relationship – I am asking them and this is significant because it changes the relationship from one where disabled people are always reacting, to one where we are pro-active. The irony in my question is clear to both parties and they are now willing to assist *me* and we both feel happy with the task.

However, it is also important to find a way to hold on to our anger where we know that it is appropriate. People offering help or asking questions is not in itself disempowering, but it is when we know that behind these questions are a whole set of assumptions about how awful the quality of our life must be and how fortunate they are not to be us. Just as difficult is the other side of this coin – the 'I think you are so wonderful, I don't know how you do it' kind of approach. Disabled people rarely, if ever, experience this as praise, unless it is said when we are actually doing something wonderful rather than just getting on with the business of living.

Our strength comes from understanding how all these responses affect and alter our perceptions of ourselves and finding ways to resist this process. To use the words of Barbara Macdonald in her discussion of how others view old people, 'If I feel shame in my lack of strength, I will have let someone else in my head for the rest of my life' (Macdonald,

1983, p. 32). We must not let other people do this to us by taking on their view of who we are and defining us by what we are incapable of doing.

It is essential to enter into dialogue with other disabled people and not allow ourselves to be isolated from the people who can help us to interpret and analyse our world. We must not think of ourselves as outsiders just because we are physically different and we need a broad, political view of the forces which are at work in these individual social encounters. Our debates with other disabled people and those non-disabled people who live and work with us and are our allies, mean that not all our dealings with the world will feel like 'encounters with strangers'.

References

Gilligan, Carol (1982) *In a Different Voice, Psychological Theory and Women's Development*, Harvard University Press.

Goffman, Erving (1956) 'On the nature of deference and demeanour', *American Anthropologist*, No. 58, pp. 473–502.

Goffman, Erving (1963) *Stigma, some notes on the management of a spoiled identity*, Penguin.

Keith, Lois (1994) 'This Week I've Been Rushed off My Wheels' in Keith, L. ed., *Mustn't Grumble: Writing by Disabled Women*, The Women's Press.

Macdonald, Barbara with Rich, Cynthia, (1983) *Look Me In The Eye: Old Women, Aging and Ageism*, The Women's Press.

Mairs, Nancy (1988) 'On Being a Cripple' in Saxton, Marsha and Howe, Florence, eds. *With Wings, An anthology of literature by women with disabilities*, Virago.

Morris, Jenny (1991) *Pride Against Prejudice: Transforming Attitudes to Disability*, The Women's Press.

Murphy, Robert (1987) *The Body Silent*, Dent.

Oliver, Michael (1990) *The Politics of Disablement*, Macmillan.

Pink, Janice (1994) 'Do Unto Others', in Keith, L. ed., *Mustn't Grumble: Writing by Disabled women*, The Women's Press.

Wates, Michele (1994) 'Self Respect', in Keith, L. ed., *Mustn't Grumble: Writing by Disabled Women*, The Women's Press.

CHAPTER FOUR

EASY TARGETS:
A Disability Rights Perspective on the 'Children as Carers' Debate

Lois Keith and Jenny Morris

Introduction

The narrator's voice sounded mournful as she read 'All their lives Jason and his sister Jamie, 16, have looked after their mother. A single parent, Theresa is partially paralysed as a result of childhood polio.' Her voice slipped down an octave as she described another mother and children, 'Eleven-year-old Stephanie and her two brothers look after the household for their mother, Christine. Christine has multiple sclerosis.'

This 50-minute documentary, called *Looking After Mum*, was shown in Channel 4's Cutting Edge series and screened at peak viewing time one week in 1994. It was part of the growing attention being given to a social issue of the 1990s, an issue summed up by 'quality' newspapers and the professional press in terms such as 'Children suffer as they care for disabled parents' (*Independent* 8 May 1992), and 'Social workers . . . have been told they must be on the look out for children shouldering the burden of caring for sick or disabled relatives at home.' (*Community Care*, 8–14 September 1994)

This chapter looks at how the children of disabled parents are being defined as 'young carers', arguing that the way in which this is happening undermines the rights of children and the rights of disabled people. We think it important to state at the outset that this is an issue which has great personal, as well as political, relevance to us for we are both disabled mothers.

The social construction of 'young carers'

The identification of 'children as carers', or 'young carers' as they have been called, is only the latest stage in a debate which has played a significant part in the development of government policy and social services practice regarding the support needed by disabled and older people living in their own homes. As feminists writing from a disability rights perspective we have, in the past, criticised the way that non-disabled feminist academics have defined family members and friends who provide help to older and disabled people as 'carers' and those they 'care for' as 'dependants'. We objected to the role of 'caring' being defined as a 'taking charge of' the person who needs practical assistance (Graham, 1983, p. 13) and to feminist researchers' silencing of the voices of those 'cared for'. We argued that by focusing on this unpaid, 'informal care' as an equal opportunities issue for (non-disabled) women, the rights of disabled and older people to adequate support which would give them choice and control in their lives has been obscured (see Morris, 1991, Chapter 6).

We have also identified how carers as a pressure group developed from being a self-help, grass roots organisation with the aim of giving women the support and confidence to refuse to act as unpaid helpers, to a professional, national organisation, funded by government, whose aim is to establish informal caring as a 'career' with a carers' income, protection of pension and other benefits (Morris, 1993, pp. 31–40). In so doing, we argued, campaigners, together with the researchers in this field, have colluded with the government's position that public resources will never be adequate to provide the support needed by older and disabled people and their insistence that 'Care *in* the community must increasingly mean care *by* the community' (Department of Health, 1981, paragraph 1.9).

The 'carers debate' itself, and the media interest in it throughout the 1980s and into the 1990s, was marked for many disabled people by the emotive terms and slogans used by those who felt that the rights and needs of 'informal carers' had not been recognised. The media posed the issue in the same terms as the academics – 'Who cares for the carers?', 'Minding the minders,' 'Who pays the cost of caring?' These were the catch phrases of the debate. The books, articles in newspapers and magazines and television programmes gave us images of dependent, usually elderly people, often apparently genderless having their slippers put on, being pushed in their wheelchairs or being fed (Keith, 1992).

If researchers and journalists could not escape working on these emotional triggers to alert the public's attention to the needs of 'carers' then it is not surprising that they sometimes go into overdrive when presenting the lives of children with disabled parents. At the time of writing this, the books and magazines on our desks include the titles, 'My child my carer,' 'My Mum needs me' and 'It's hard work looking after Mum'. The first of these is the title of an academic research paper, the second a book aimed at all those involved with children in families where a parent is ill or disabled, and the third a newspaper article in the 'serious' press.

While the issue of 'young carers' has become of increasing public and policy interest, the research which has highlighted their existence has so far been small-scale and, for us, raises more questions than it answers. In terms of numbers of children involved there is very little in the way of hard evidence. The Carers' National Association has suggested that there might be 10,000 'young carers' in the country, whilst Gillian Parker estimates that as many as 68,000 children under the age of 16 have been providing 'care' to their parents (Parker, 1994, p. 9). More recently, Crossroads Care Association trumpeted that 'Estimates reveal over 20,000 young people caring for dependent family members' (Press Release 18 November 1994).

The research studies of, the campaigning on, and the media interest in 'young carers' have tended to repeat two things which were common to the earlier debate and research on carers generally. They have defined and named a role ('young carers') which, until the children and young people came into contact with researchers or professionals, was not how they described themselves. And secondly, both researchers, campaigners and journalists alike have defined the main policy issue to be that of providing services to 'young carers' which would ease the 'burden of caring'. We want to consider these two aspects of the debate before going on to provide an alternative perspective from the point of view of disabled parents.

A reversal of roles?

While the varied statistical estimates of the number of 'young carers' create confusion so too does the use of the words 'care' and 'carers'. Research and policy development on 'carers' generally has assumed that this social issue concerns a relationship where one party, the 'carer' takes responsibility for another, the 'dependent relative'. Using the words 'young carers' therefore assumes that we are talking about a situation where a child or young person is taking responsibility for an adult, usually their parent – and that a reversal of roles is therefore involved, with the child 'parenting' the parent.

There are a handful of small-scale studies which address the question of what tasks children of disabled or chronically ill parents might have to perform and the emotional and practical consequences for both parents and child, but these are predominantly anecdotal and poorly designed. The Tameside Study (O'Neill, 1988), and the Sandwell Study (Page, 1988), were both criticised by later researchers such as Aldridge and Becker (1993) for not providing any understanding of what 'young carers' are saying about their lives and needs. However Aldridge and Becker's own research in Nottingham which sets out to 'develop a specific analytical model to assist under-standing of the young carer's roles and needs' (p. 6) was derived from an opportunistic sample of 15 children one of whom was a three-year-old whose 'caring' tasks for her grandmother were described by her own parent.

Whilst these researchers revealed some interesting anec-dotal evidence about the lives of the young people they questioned, they frequently chose to use terms to describe the children that the respondents were unwilling to use to describe themselves. Indeed, they seem to have imposed their own defintions and perceptions on the subjects of their research. Sandra Bilsborrow's Merseyside study (Bilsborrow, 1992) is one such example. In this study she interviewed 11 young people who she identified as providing help to a disabled or ill relative. Her section on 'The young carer's perspective', includes the heading 'The care needs of the dependent relative', even though none of the children in her study referred to 'care needs' or to the 'dependent relative'. Instead they talked about actual tasks like shopping, cleaning and cooking for 'my mum' (all but one of the respondents was helping their mother).

Aldridge and Becker (1993, p. 58) say that they have not used the term 'dependent' in their report since none of the children in their study used it but then none of these young people used the words 'care provider' to describe themselves or 'care receiver' to describe their parents or relatives, yet these are the terms the researchers consistently use. This gives rise to considerable confusion about the question which for many researchers is at the centre of this debate about 'children who care', namely: 'Who is doing the parenting?' Or 'Have disabled parents and their children exchanged roles?'

The idea of children having to 'parent their parents' or 'swap roles' seems to fascinate researchers and journalists alike and is an important part of most portrayals of the lives of families where a parent is ill or disabled. This fascination colours the researcher's or journalist's perspective even when it is contradicted by the children's understanding of their lives. Aldridge and Becker for example, talk about children for whom 'the roles have been reversed so that the child becomes the parent of the parent' but then go on to say that 'even though the child has undertaken caring responsibility for the parent, their [i.e. the parent's] existence in the home as parental figures is crucial' (p. 58).

These researchers seem reluctant to jettison the notion of 'role reversal' even when their evidence fails to back it up. Thus, Aldridge and Becker write:

> None of the child or adult carers talked about the care receiver in terms of dependency. Pragamatically the role

might have been reversed, but emotionally their parents' status as guardians remained intact. This could explain why young carers demonstrated such a high level of commitment to their parents and why the loss of a parent was not of immediate psychological benefit to the young carer. [sic] Thus we can see that the young carers' burden of responsibility was only a practical responsibility, and not a burden in terms of their emotional and psychological relationship with their parents. (Aldridge and Becker, 1993, p. 58)

Yet their research is summarised as 'an account of choice and responsibility turned upside down: of children having to perform the most basic, personal and intimate tasks, becoming their parent's parent . . .'

To us, it seems that the reluctance of these and other researchers to give up the notion of children 'parenting their parents' is created by the way that 'caring' as taking responsibility for someone is linked to the provision of help with certain personal care tasks. Aldridge and Becker neatly illustrate this link when they ask 'at what age should it be acceptable for a person (child) to take *responsibility* for the care of their parent – for toileting them, for showering them or for dispensing medications?' (1994, p. 33)

The Independent Living Movement challenges the assumption that to receive help with personal care tasks is necessarily to become dependent, to have someone taking responsibility for you (see Morris, 1993, Chapter 2). If a person who needs such help maintains control over how the help is provided then they retain their independence and their responsibility for themselves. Research studies on 'young carers' assume too readily that receiving help with personal care tasks involves giving over responsibility for oneself to someone else – thus the assumption that in this kind of situation a child is parenting their parent.

Moreover, much of the thinking around the issue of children who are 'carers' has difficulty distinguishing between parenting – the concern and sense of responsibility that parents have for their children's welfare in all its manifestations – and the practical and physical things which adults do when looking after children and running a home, a point also made by Gillian Parker (Parker, 1994). Whilst the academic research and television documentaries such as *Looking After Mum* actually contain little evidence of children 'parenting their parents' – although much evidence of children having to carry out a number of practical and sometimes personal care tasks because of the lack of alternative help – researchers and journalists alike seem unable to refrain from presenting this kind of picture of households where a parent is ill or disabled.

Parents who become ill or disabled in the course of parenting may need help in retaining or regaining confidence in their ability to continue to do this job well, but those involved in researching these issues perhaps need reminding that a disabled parent's ability to love and care for their children is not dependent on them being able to perform all the physical tasks that other parents might do. Furthermore, whilst a physical impairment does not affect a parent's desire to perform this role, the lack of appropriate housing or adequate support services may well limit what they can do for themselves and what they have to ask other family members to do for them (see Morris, 1993, Chapter 6).

As Gillian Parker says in her paper *Where Next for Research on Carers?* (1994): 'While it seems true that children with disabled parents sometimes find themselves carrying a level of responsibility in excess of that of their peers, they do this because their parents are inadequately supported, not necessarily because their parents are disabled.'

If impairment or illness in itself is assumed to create a situation where a parent cannot retain responsibility for their children so that children are required to give, not just practical or personal assistance to the parent, but also make the kind of decisions parents normally make, the consequences can be significant for both parent and child alike, as we shall see.

'Easing the burden of caring'

We would argue that, generally, the social issue of 'caring' has been constructed and based on the assumption that the unpaid work within the family of those identified as 'carers' will continue and that central and local government should develop policies and practices to support this work. Colluding with the government's position that public resources will never be adequate to replace the practical assistance given within the family (mainly by women) to disabled and older people, many researchers and campaigners have focused on the provision of services which would 'ease the burden of caring'. In practice, this has meant services such as: 'respite care' (that is, short-term breaks from 'caring' for the 'carer', which often involve the disabled person going into residential care); equipment to ease the physical tasks of lifting and so on; support groups for 'carers'. Within this framework, disabled and older people are 'dependants', their partners, relatives, friends become their 'carers', and the only situation in which the 'burden of caring' is abolished altogether is where they are admitted into residential care – or where a 'young carer' is removed from his/her family.

Just as in the work on adult carers, researchers and campaigners have insisted that the role of 'young carers' should be recognised and the needs created by this role addressed. We would not deny, that where *both* parent and child/young person *prefer* practical assistance to be given within the parent/child relationship, this may be acceptable (depending on the tasks concerned, a point we discuss later) and the child's role may well mean that s/he has support needs which should be met. However, we would argue that, in most circumstances, if the focus was instead on the needs for practical assistance and personal care experienced by the parent, the child's right to unimpeded educational and social opportunities is more likely to be protected and their emotional well-being promoted.

In contrast, some researchers on 'young carers' express concern that 'professional support was aimed specifically at the care receiver rather than young carers'. (Aldridge and Becker, 1993, p. 36) They go on to argue that 'Not one professional agency had engaged the young carers in any discussion about their caring responsibilities, experiences or needs', and that 'at no time did the social workers talk to the young carers about their caring roles' (p. 39).

Whilst it is important and sometimes vital to recognise young people's need to talk about the difficulties of their lives, to us it seems wholly appropriate that it is the *parent* who should be consulted about the support to be provided by community care assistants, nurses, doctors and social workers. This is not because we want to maintain what Aldridge and Becker describe as 'the veil of silence surrounding the young caring experience' (p. 37) but because we believe that in the vast majority of cases, the parent is both willing and capable of making decisions about the organisation of the family. Where appropriate services are provided for the family member who needs assistance, it is much more likely that the child or young adult can get on with the ordinary business of growing up.

In fact, evidence (including that of Aldridge and Becker's research) suggests that service providers do in fact recognise that children and young people provide practical assistance and sometimes personal care for their parents. Unfortunately, this recognition usually takes the form of assuming that children and young people will actually carry out tasks of housework, shopping and help with personal care when their parent is ill or disabled. Recognition of the role of 'young carers' is not enough therefore, unless it goes hand in hand with ensuring that support is provided to a disabled or ill parent from alternative sources.

Most importantly, none of the research on 'young carers' identifies that disabled people have a statutory right to have their needs for support assessed and for those assessed needs (including the need for practical assistance and for aids, adaptations and equipment) to be met. A statutory duty is imposed on social services authorities to carry out such assessments by the 1986 Disabled Persons Act and to meet such assessed needs by the 1970 Chronically Sick and Disabled Persons Act. Focusing on the needs of children and young people which are created by the fact that they provide assistance to a parent merely serves to obscure these rights and thereby reinforces the need for help to be provided within the family.

How do we see it?

As disabled mothers we have a vested interest in this debate: our children are not our 'carers', they do not parent us; but the social construction of 'young carers' and the media attention which has followed affects us every time we go out with our children, every time we meet new people, especially health and social services professionals. The research and media presentation of 'children as carers' undermines our role as mothers and defines disabled parents as inadequate.

We also have an interest in the issue from our children's point of view, because, if we need help we do not wish our children to be forced into providing levels of support which it is inappropriate for a child to provide for his/her parents and which thereby damage the child's emotional and physical well-being, their educational and social development.

Interestingly, during the same period that 'young carers' have been defined and their needs addressed within a social agenda, disabled parents themselves have become more visible and vocal in defining both their rights to be parents and the support they sometimes need in this role (Gradwell, 1992; Morris, 1989; Morris, 1992; Mason, 1992).

As disabled mothers, we feel our interests, and those of our children, are better reflected by the kind of research and recommendations made by the Maternity Alliance (1993a and b) and Shackle (1993) than by those associated with the 'carers' lobby'. This is hardly surprising for the Maternity Alliance's publications have resulted from working in partnership with disabled parents, taking the lead from how disabled people define their experiences and interests. In particular, whereas the 'carers' lobby' has identified the personal assistance needs of disabled and ill parents in terms of their 'dependency' on family and friends, the Maternity Alliance has followed the disabled people's movement in defining personal assistance needs in terms of independent living. In other words, it has been defined in terms of the need for people to be able to exert choice and control over how personal assistance is delivered. Thus, the *Charter for Disabled Parents and Parents-to-be* which resulted from their joint working with disabled parents addressed how independent living could be promoted, stressing

> Our vision is of a society in which services are flexible enough to meet individual needs as defined by parents themselves. In addition, the need to make adaptations around the house, buy in special equipment or pay for additional domestic help, for example, imposes extra financial burdens upon disabled parents which will be recognised and adequately financially supported. (Maternity Alliance, 1993b)

While the Maternity Alliance research and recommendations focused on the promotion of independence for the disabled parent, many of their findings about the disabling attitudes and inadequacies of service provision reflects that of the 'children as carers' research. Each type of research is therefore addressing and describing the same reality; the difference is in how this reality – and the relationships associated with it – are defined, how the associated needs are recognised and the policy recommendations which result.

We want to analyse the situation facing disabled parents and their children from the point of view of the disabling barriers they experience. However, we also want to give full recognition to the rights of children. The next two sections of this chapter therefore address these two issues.

What creates a disabled parent's need for support from children/young people within a family?

Notwithstanding the difficulties which are sometimes an inherent part of impairment and illness, there are in fact a number of factors which are more important than illness or impairment itself in determining both the need for support and the difficulties experienced in getting the right kind of support in the most appropriate way. These disabling barriers in themselves create a need to rely on family and friends.

Poverty

Impairment and illness often bring unemployment and

reduced earning power. Those who are born with an impairment may experience segregated education and discrimination when they try to enter the labour market. Those who acquire an impairment in adult life are at high risk of losing employment and are often unable to re-enter the labour market. The government's own survey of disabled people found that only 31 per cent of adults below retirement age were in employment (Martin and White, 1988). Impairment and illness bring higher daily living costs and this, combined with low income, can create real barriers to independent living.

Poverty means that when disabled people need practical assistance and personal care they will rely on family, friends and the state. The care component of the Disability Living Allowance is not sufficient to purchase more than a few hours help per week and only a small proportion of disabled people qualify for cash payments under the quite stringent means-testing of the Independent Living Fund (a situation which is unlikely to change under any future system of direct payments to be introduced). Assessment of need carried out by social services care managers is rarely based on independent living principles and often assumes that unpaid help of family members will be available – indeed care managers usually have to make this assumption because of the demands on their budgets.

Research on 'young carers' has also recognised the effect of poverty, although there the association between low income and inability to get appropriate help from outside the family is posed in terms of children/young people feeling that they have 'no choice' over helping their parent(s). Aldridge and Becker found that 'The majority of the young carers interviewed experienced economic privations. Their families were either living off one wage, or social security benefits . . .' (1993, p. 16). They argue that 'Young carers are effectively denied the prospect of choice and often circumstances (usually socio economic) prevail in the home to prevent the activation of caring alternatives' (p. 17).

It is probably no accident that many of the children portrayed by the media as 'caring' for their parents are in fact living in a single parent household, although we cannot generalise as neither these portrayals nor the existing small-scale research can be said to be representative of 'young carers'. Nevertheless, the association of single parenthood with poverty, together with the absence of another adult who may provide an alternative source of help may well mean that single parents are at greater risk of having to rely on their children.

Disabling professional attitudes

A lack of personal purchasing power may mean that a disabled parent needs to turn to his/her local authority social services department for help yet sometimes professional attitudes can deter disabled parents from asking for the support they need.

The Maternity Alliance's research, published as *Mother's Pride and Others' Prejudice*, highlighted the way that attitudes held by health and social services professionals can make disabled parents reluctant to ask for support. One woman said, 'The social worker threatened to take my baby off me because she did not think I was capable of looking after him by myself. But I am glad to say four years on I have proved her wrong' (Maternity Alliance, 1993a, p. 18). Another mother said that although she repeatedly requested information and asked to see a neurologist the only response was that the health visitor said 'I could be classified as an unfit mother due to my multiple sclerosis' (p. 18). Some mothers at the Maternity Alliance's conference revealed a 'fear of having their child removed. This fear made them reluctant to ask for help from the social services department in case any request was interpreted as inability to cope' (Shackle, 1993, p. 10).

This fear seems justified: 'Gwen explained that after her accident [a hit and run accident which resulted in paraplegia] she was deserted by her husband and lost custody of her daughter because the judge doubted the quality of the home life she could offer. "... I had a phone call with my daughter for ten minutes a week and holidays together only when we could afford them. Even the holidays were difficult because it was insisted on that I had a carer with me in case I had an accident, even though for the remaining 300 days of the year I didn't have a carer" (Shackle, 1993, p. 13).

And a couple who are both disabled found their abilities as parents were questioned. 'After the birth, [they] experienced great difficulty getting discharged from hospital with [their son] "It wasn't just a matter of asking the sister if it was okay to go home, it wasn't a case of checking with the obstetrician or paediatrician but rather a case of "we'll wait and see what social services say" 'They were very worried that a care order would be placed on Christopher which made it difficult to raise complaints about the way in which they were treated. For instance, when they consulted a solicitor about the continuous interrogation by their health visitor, he advised them not to upset her as she might bring in the social services department' (Shackle, 1993, p. 15).

Again, research which focuses on 'young carers' also reflects the effect of disabling attitudes. When Aldridge and Becker interviewed the parents of the young people in their survey they found that parents' fear of their child(ren) being taken away often deterred them from asking for help. As one woman said, 'Of course I had a fear. I tell you, one big fear I had and it was horrific. I wouldn't accept any help from the services, the likes of home help, I was terrified if they took her off me. I was terrified in case they'd say, "because of your illness, because of everything, you're not capable of looking after her, you're not," and I daren't say anything. I daren't let them know how I was feeling or how she was feeling.' And another woman said 'Disabled people hide it [the fact that they need help] because they're frightened of losing their kids. I didn't contact any professionals because of that.' (Aldridge and Becker, 1994, p. 10.)

Disabling services
The experiences discussed above make it more likely that disabled and ill parents will rely on family and friends for help. They are also pressurised into doing this when professionals offer inappropriate or inadequate help. This is unfortunately all too common an experience (see Morris, 1993).

The Maternity Alliance's research, for example, found that

health and social services often have little knowledge of disabled parents and their needs. 'The occupational therapist who came to see me hadn't come across my situation before so it was a case of my telling her the areas I found difficult and her suggesting ways round them' (Maternity Alliance, 1993a, p. 19). One woman said that her 'OT seems to be reinventing the wheel – aids designed from scratch – I can't believe other areas have never come across problems before – why can't they share solutions?' And another woman said 'I was visited by a health visitor and midwife which I found helpful regarding the baby but there was no help for me regarding how a diabetic mother should cope, and problems that occured because of the condition' (p. 20). Such experiences can be disconcerting and a resulting anger with inadequate professional help makes reliance on family and friends more likely.

A lack of knowledge about the needs of disabled parents – about their experience from their point of view – partly explains the fact that when services are available they are often delivered in ways which are inappropriate and/or disempowering.

One woman described the mismatch between what kind of help would have suited her and her daughter and that which was actually available: 'When I had to go into hospital because my back went, I was ill for six weeks and both E. and I needed 24-hour support. It cost me £640 which I couldn't afford . . . I rang social services to ask if I could have any financial help towards the cost – but they said no, but E. could go in a foster home! This was an intolerable option to me. I asked if I could have the money they would have paid the foster parents, to pay for care in our home, on my terms, and they said no' (Maternity Alliance, 1993a, p. 20).

Other women have described how, even when help *is* available from a social services department, it can be difficult to persuade the helper to do the tasks which they wanted done. Some of the women attending the Maternity Alliance's Conference shared their experiences of how helpers have a tendency to take over the care of the child instead of giving support to parents which would enable them to manage childcare tasks themselves (Shackle, 1993, p. 10). Other people find that home helps will not do the tasks which they want doing and this often makes parents reliant on children or other members of the family. As one woman said, 'I was allowed a home help to take my son to school but they wouldn't do any housework for me as there were others in the house in the evening. This meant my son had to do most things for me' (Maternity Alliance, 1993a, p. 20).

Research on 'young carers' found the same experience and highlighted that statutory services commonly identify family members (including children) as carers and see them as service providers whose presence means that scarce public resources are not allocated. The Merseyside research, for example, described one such situation where a young person was identified as the sole carer of a parent with a physical impairment. 'The social worker referred the family to the home help service. The home help was to visit the family to offer help in the mornings. This service was withdrawn after a short period as the young carer was considered able to perform the tasks which the home help was doing' (Bilsborrow, 1992, p. 19).

The Nottingham research found that statutory services assume that children will start to perform practical tasks at a certain age – for example, Community Care Assistants were withdrawn when children reach an age where it was considered appropriate that they helped their disabled parent – which varied from between 12 and 16 years of age (Aldridge and Becker, 1994, p. 5) As one mother said, 'They just said they couldn't spare the help any more because they thought the children would be able to cope . . . this is going back nearly three years, so the eldest one must have been about 12 and the youngest was about nine . . . but we don't like to put too much on the youngest one, he suffers with asthma' (1994, p. 5).

Even when services are available they are often delivered in ways which create a need for a young person to help, or assume that the help of the young person will supplement that provided by the paid carer. As one child said, 'Sometimes when I go to school in the morning [the care worker] says can you come home at dinner so I can go out and get some things' (Bilsborrow, 1992, p. 32).

A need to rely on family members, including children, is therefore created by the way that social services departments allocate their resources and deliver their services.

Services which are culturally insensitive can also part- icularly create the need to rely on family members amongst ethnic minority communities. A workshop on this issue at the Maternity Alliance's Conference reported how the needs of disabled parents from Asian communities are unrecognised and unmet. 'More social workers, counsellors, community workers, home helps, midwives and others from minority ethnic groups speaking their language, would enable parents to feel more free to express their needs and problems and seek further advice from service providers . . . Particular attention needs to be paid to developing communication stategies with disabled people who do not understand English. Very few signers in this country can sign in foreign languages' (Shackle, 1993, p. 11).

People from all backgrounds will be pushed into relying on the help of family and friends if little choice is available in terms of the kind of help statutory services will provide or the individuals who will come into their homes. The latter point is important – people need to trust those who necessarily 'intrude into their families' and their own personal privacy. Particular difficulties in this area are experienced by black and ethnic minority people: 'In the Asian families the lack of religious/racial compatibility, the lack of cultural under- standing, and the disregard for the families' expressed needs was particularly pronounced' (Aldridge and Becker, 1994, p. 7).

Disabling environments
The research on 'young carers' also revealed examples of inaccessible housing creating a need for help. One child interviewed by Aldridge and Becker talked of how she had to stay off school in order to help her mother up and down stairs to the toilet. Her mother reported how she had applied to the council to be rehoused in a bungalow so that she wouldn't have to keep her daughter off school in order to provide her with the help she needed. However, the council had said

they didn't have a bungalow big enough for her family and the only further response from statutory agencies was that the education authority threatened to take her to court because her daughter was missing school.

Disabled parents are particularly affected by the stereo-typical assumptions which for years dictated that, when local authority and housing associations built to wheelchair standard, they tended to build one bedroom properties, rather than family-size properties.

An inaccessible environment generally creates a greater need for help. For example, if shops, libraries, post offices, public transport and so on are not accessible to people with mobility impairments then someone else has to get the family's shopping, change library books, and cash benefits. If printed material is not available in large print, Braille or on tape then those with visual impairments must rely on others, while a lack of induction loops or Sign Language Interpreters will similarly disable Deaf or hard of hearing people.

The removal of such barriers would make a considerable difference to most disabled people's lives and illustrate how inappropriate it is to define our needs to be for 'care' rather than for civil rights.

Disabling experiences and disabling communities

Women who have grown up with physical or sensory impairment or a learning difficulty often find that they do not have the opportunity to develop caring skills, particularly if they experience segregated education and residential provision where the emphasis is on their protection rather than a promotion of independence. 'Micheline felt that her caring skills were underdeveloped during the early part of her life. When she first left home and school she felt she would not be able to look after herself, let alone anybody else. 'I didn't even have the confidence to think I could keep a pot plant alive!' However, she did and moved on to greater things. 'When the busy lizzie lived I moved on to Tweety-Pie the canary' (Shackle, 1993, p. 4).

Negative images of disabled people undermine people's identity as parents. 'Images of disabled people as parents and grandparents are notable for their rarity. The 'giving' image of the parent and the 'dependent' image of disabled people do not mix easily' (Shackle, 1993, p. 7). In a workshop on images of disabled parents, several disabled people reported how they had themselves been photographed as parents by the media. 'Everyone felt that the pictures had in some sense misrepresented their experience; by concentrating on their personal story when actually they were trying to get a social issue across or by insisting on showing the media's idea of the disabled parent as isolated, heroic and vulnerable instead of looking at the actual experience of the family concerned' (p. 7).

Negative images, segregation, discrimination – there are all part of the every-day experiences of disabled children and adults. Living in a society which does not value disabled people, where to be ill or different is to be set apart, means living in a community which does not offer the kind of support which empowers people.

The 'young carers' research illustrated some of the consequences of this when children and young people described the prejudice they experienced towards their disabled parents – 'They call her a cripple and all that and it upsets me' (Bilsborrow, 1992, p. 34). Segregation of disabled people generally from mainstream social and economic life means that many non-disabled people have little knowledge or understanding of impairment – this compounds the minority experience of children of disabled parents and adds to their isolation – 'I can't talk to my friends because they don't understand . . .' (Bilsborrow, 1992, p. 35).

The Nottingham research found that families with a disabled or ill parent were rarely offered support from the community in which they lived. 'This coincides with earlier findings that people – even family members – tend to shy away or avoid illness and any sort of commitment to families where illness or disability is present. Perhaps because they are wary of becoming involved as they're uncertain of the level of commitment they may have to give. Or perhaps simply because they do not want to commit any time to a family that so clearly *needs* help' (Aldridge and Becker, 1994, p. 3).

And sometimes parents and children experience outright

hostility. As one young girl said, 'People round here, they are always picking on people if you've got something wrong with your mum' (Aldridge and Becker, 1993, p. 5).

The effect of wider social attitudes is also apparent in assumptions about men and women's roles. Ideas about what men and women do and how they relate to each other can create a situation in which a husband does not offer much help to his wife if she is ill or disabled, or indeed abandons her because she no longer fulfills the role society in general tells him to expect. This in itself can create a situation where children have to provide help.

Miriam, for example, described her father's refusal to help in terms of his feeling that his wife no longer fulfilled the role he expected of her. 'He finds it hard to face, I know because he once said he had lost his wife, he hadn't got a wife who could stand beside him in the pub. He sees other men out with their wives but he wouldn't think of taking her out in the wheel-chair' (Aldridge and Becker, 1993, p. 32).

Children's rights and family life

We have seen that there are a number of factors commonly experienced by disabled and ill parents which can create the need for them to rely on their children for practical help. We have also argued that the research and policy agenda which defines the children of ill or disabled parents as 'young carers' does not reflect the reality as defined by parent or child. In fact – in so constructing the role – researchers and policy-makers collude with the pressure on families to cope with the personal assistance requirements of their members with the minimum of outside help.

Defining children of disabled or ill parents as 'young carers' not only undermines the parent/child relationship, it also fudges the issue of whether children *should* be performing such personal assistance tasks. It needs to be clearly stated that it is not acceptable for children of disabled or ill parents to carry out tasks which adversely affect their emotional, social and educational development. Indeed, the parents interviewed by Aldridge and Becker in their follow-up study, all stated that they found this unacceptable (Aldridge and Becker, 1994,

p. 32). That such situations exist is a reflection of the social and economic disadvantages which accompany illness and impairment and which can only be addressed by removing the kind of disabling barriers we have already identified.

However, as disabled parents we are all too aware how quick other people are to assume, unjustifiably, that our children 'look after' us. While it is important to establish what is inappropriate, unfair or even dangerous to ask children to do for disabled or ill parents, the discussion needs to take account of what is generally regarded as appropriate responsibilities for children at various ages.

As Gillian Parker says,

> Research in this area would necessarily have to engage in a debate about what any children in any family do for each other and for their parents. Only then could assertions about undue responsibility being laid on the shoulders of 'child carers' be made. (Parker, 1994, p. 10)

Perhaps this issue would not seem so contentious for disabled people if the debate always took place in the context of serious discussion and research about the rights of children and young people. Unfortunately, in the hands of many television producers and newspaper journalists, disabled parents are easy targets for the accusation that, if we can't do it all on our own, we are incapable of doing our job properly. Indeed, sometimes the very idea of disabled people having children is seen as exploitative.

Disabled people can be used as targets in this way and have to accept that our children are described as 'little angels' who are forced to 'neglect their schoolwork and friends' in order to look after us. However, children from other families who may be asked to take on responsibilities that some adults with a more 'child-centred' approach (some would read this as meaning white and middle-class) would see as burdensome or exploitative are not exposed to the same treatment.

For example, in our work in education, we have often come across situations where children are expected to perform tasks in families which mean that they are denied certain freedom of choice in their social and educational lives which other groups in society may feel should be part of universal children's rights. Some young people in secondary schools, particularly girls, are not allowed to take part in clubs, school plays or sporting activities which involve staying after school because they are expected to pick up a younger sibling or regularly peform tasks like cooking and cleaning at home. Some children take time off school to translate for their parents at the council or at the doctor's. Others are limited in their choice of higher education because they are expected to carry on living at home, taking quite serious family responsibilities. Other groups might feel uncomfortable about these restrictions on children's lives, but these issues have not become part of a condemnatory public debate in the way that families which have a disabled parent have done because it has been assumed that there are differences between families and that it is not always appropriate to say to the parents of other cultural and social groups, 'you should not be allowed to do that to your children, you are denying them their rights'.

However, although it is important to understand that different families view childhood and its freedoms in different ways, it is important to establish what, if anything, it is unacceptable to ask a child or young person to do. Aldridge and Becker isolate different caring tasks and responsibilities and of those, the tasks that seemed the easiest to say 'children should never be asked to do this', are the ones which involved the heavy lifting of adults and those intimate personal tasks such as bathing, toileting, wiping and dressing which were distressing and embarrassing to both the parent and the child and meant that the parent was denied privacy and dignity.

The choice both parent and child have in these circumstances is often dependent on access to external support, accessible housing and appropriate aids and equipment. Where accessible accommodation is provided, a child is far less likely to have to lift a heavy adult. Where appropriate support is given, a child will not have to perform intimate tasks which neither party wants them to have to do. We feel that campaigners and researchers alike should focus more clearly on what needs to be done to prevent parents having to rely on their children for such tasks. In particular, they should focus on how disabled people can access the clear rights that they already have under existing legislation to practical assistance, aids, adaptations and equipment.

Other tasks such as cooking, housework, shopping, assisting a parent out of doors may be onerous if the child is asked to do them all the time but it is important not to stigmatise parents and children as 'dependants and young carers' merely because the parent is ill or disabled. The Channel 4 documentary which we mentioned at the beginning of this chapter, characterised a disabled woman's children as 'looking after Mum' by filming the family doing the weekly supermarket shopping. Christine may have been sending her children off down the aisles to get cat food because she could not walk far but the situation portrayed was not very different from the weekly shopping trips of millions of other families where a parent is *not* ill or disabled. It was all too easy for the programme makers to present the families' difficulties as entirely stemming from the fact that Christine has multiple sclerosis. The reality was that, like most mothers, she was driven up the wall by her children's ability to create a drawerful of odd socks and that, like many children of divorcing parents, they were caught in the middle of a conflict between their parents which was obviously quite emotionally damaging.

Researchers and journalists alike should beware of labelling relationships and tasks where a parent is ill or disabled as entirely created by impairment or illness. Such a practice can only lead to stereotyping and stigmatising disabled parents and their children alike and does little to promote the human and civil rights of either.

Conclusion

The identification of 'children as carers' has far-reaching, and potentially devastating, consequences for many disabled and/or ill parents. Researchers and the Carers' National Association have focused on the help that children and young people who are identified as 'carers' need in order to carry on this role. The media have tended to focus on the 'burden' experienced by these children and explicity or implicitly questioned whether they should be allowed to remain with their parents. Neither approach identifies the support that a disabled or ill parent might need as the issue. As we conclude this chapter, radio, television and newspaper headlines are highlighting the plight of a seven-year-old who sat by her mother's body for two days after she died from Lupus, a disorder of the immune system. Charlotte had been placed with foster parents but was allowed back home because, as a social services spokesman said, her mother 'could not bear to be apart from her all the time and wanted to see Charlotte at weekends' (*The Independent*, 23 December 1994). The question the media are asking is not – why wasn't this woman given sufficient support but why was Charlotte allowed back home with her mother?

This is the fear that all disabled or ill parents live with: are we considered to be good enough parents and if not is someone going to 'rescue' our child/ren from the 'burden' of having a disabled or ill parent? We feel it to varying degrees – mainly determined by what material resources we have and whether we have partners or extended family on whose support we can rely. The 'young carers' issue is, to a considerable extent, an issue for single parents – the majority of whom are women. It is no accident that the Channel 4 documentary referred to in this chapter was entirely about the lives of disabled single, separated or divorced mothers. Yet this was not commented upon by any of the extensive press coverage which accompanied the programme. Neither has the correlation between children having to provide a high level of practical assistance to a disabled parent and the likelihood of these parents being single mothers been remarked upon by researchers in this field. The particular difficulties experienced by single disabled mothers and the way that the debate on 'young carers' has fed into the debate on single parents – both of them containing an implicit if not explicit attack on women's ability to parent without the presence of a man in the household – remains an unexplored, but important, issue.

However, we are all, disabled men and women, married,

divorced or single, undermined as parents by the political, academic and media representation of 'children as carers'. At the very least, all disabled parents experience the assumption of strangers that our children 'look after' us. More seriously, those who have little money or access to support from family and friends are at the mercy of judgements to be made by social services professionals about whether we can be adequate parents. To ask for help is often interpreted as an inability to parent and there is a genuine fear held by both parents and children that it is better to keep silent about any difficulties because of the fear that the children will be taken into care.

We are easy targets in a society where to be disabled is to be segregated, institutionalised, denied autonomy, discriminated against. A society where charitable benevolence is the best we can expect, while revulsion and fear are never far from the surface. In this society, children of disabled parents are 'children of courage', 'little angels' whose caring is applauded until some line is crossed – which varies according to a number of factors, including media interest. At that point, the question all too often is not, 'How can this parent be supported?' but 'Does the situation warrant our taking this child out of his/her home?' Or placing the parent in a Home?

By constructing children as 'carers', both researchers and the Carers' National Association have failed to address the question of how disabled parents can access their rights, under the 1970 Chronically Sick and Disabled Persons Act, to practical assistance, aids, adaptations and equipment. Appropriate support for the disabled parent is often the best way to ensure the rights of the child promoted by the Children Act 1989, such as the right to a childhood which is safe and protected. These organisations have, instead, colluded with the assumptions underpinning the implementation of the 1990 NHS and Community Care Act – namely that, to quote its architect, families, friends and neighbours would 'continue to be the primary means by which people are enabled to live normal lives in community settings'. (Griffiths, 1988, para 3.2)

References

Aldridge, Jo and Becker, Paul (1993) *Children Who Care: Inside the world of young carers*, Department of Social Sciences, Loughborough University.

Aldridge, Jo and Becker, Paul (1994) *My Child My Carer: The parents' perspective*, Department of Social Sciences, Loughborough University.

Bilsborrow, Sandra (1992) *You Grow Up Fast As Well . . . Young Carers on Merseyside*, Barnado's.

Department of Health and Social Security (1981) *Growing Older*, HMSO.

Gradwell, Lorraine (1992) 'The parent's tale', in *Coalition*, September, pp. 17–19.

Graham, Hilary (1983) 'Caring: a labour of love' in Finch, Janet and Groves, Dulcie, *A Labour of Love – Women, Work and Caring*, Routledge & Kegan Paul.

Griffiths, Roy (1988) *Community Care: An agenda for action*, HMSO.

Keith, Lois (1992) 'Who cares wins? Women, caring and disability', in *Disability, Handicap and Society*, Vol. 7, No. 2, pp. 167–75.

Martin, Jean and White, Amanda (1988) *The Financial Circumstances of Disabled Adults Living in Private Households*, HMSO.

Mason, Micheline (1992) 'A nineteen parent family' in Morris, Jenny, ed., *Alone Together: Voices of single mothers*, The Women's Press.

Maternity Alliance (1993a) *Mothers Pride and Others' Prejudice: A survey of disabled mothers' experience of maternity*, Maternity Alliance.

Maternity Alliance (1993b) *Listen To Us For a Change: A charter for disabled parents and parents-to-be*, The Maternity Alliance.

Morris, Jenny, ed., (1989) *Able Lives: Women's Experience of Paralysis*, The Women's Press.

Morris, Jenny (1991) *Pride Against Prejudice: Transforming Attitudes to Disability*, The Women's Press.

Morris, Jenny (1992) 'Feeling special', in Morris, Jenny ed., *Alone Together: Voices of Single Mothers*, The Women's Press.

Morris, Jenny (1993) *Independent Lives? Community Care and Disabled People*, Macmillan.

O'Neill, A. (1988) *Young Carers: The Tameside research*, Tameside Metropolitan Borough Council.

Page, R. (1988) *Report on the Initial Survey Investigating the Number of Young Carers in Sandwell Secondary Schools*, Sandwell Metropolitan Borough Council.

Parker, Gillian (1989) *Where Next for Research on Carers?* Nuffield Community Care Studies Unit, Leicester University.

Shackle, Mary (1993) *I Thought I Was the Only One: / report of a conference 'Disabled People, Pregnancy and Early Parenthood'*, Maternity Alliance.

CHAPTER FIVE

SEXUAL ABUSE AND DISABLED CHILDREN
Margaret Kennedy

We need to have confidence in our ability to read and interpret. Rather than believe in 'experts' who imply they know it all, we must look for the gaps and hidden agendas. If knowledge and power go hand in hand, it is the responsibility of feminists both to acquire knowledge and to transform it.
(Cameron and Fraser, 1987)

In the last few years there has been a surge of recognition and concern about the sexual abuse of disabled children. This concern has been slow to come and has certainly lagged behind efforts to protect non-disabled children. This chapter provides an overview of the current state of knowledge and thinking, and identifies some issues surrounding the future development of work in this field.

Definitions
Guidance issued on the implementation of the Children Act 1989 defines four categories of abuse: neglect, physical injury, sexual abuse and emotional abuse. However, some feminist writers such as Liz Kelly, have stressed that it is important to include the child's subjective experience as part of the definition of abuse (Kelly, 1988). Children who are abused may not experience things in quite the same way as professionals and policy-makers suggest in their categorisation of abuse.

In recent years, disabled people and their organisations have challenged definitions of abuse generally, highlighting the way that society's reactions to impairments have both constituted and resulted in abuse. They have argued that official definitions of physical and emotional abuse and neglect fail to encompass a full range of abusive experiences that disabled adults speak about.

In particular, they have argued, abuse is not simply defined by what happens, but by how it is experienced. This is an important point to make in the context of what disabled people have defined as 'abusive practices'. This term refers to professional, institutional and social practices which have been a 'taken for granted' part of disabled children's/adult's lives but which are experienced by individuals as abuse.

The British Association for the Study and Prevention of Child Abuse and Neglect (BASPCAN) carried out a working party study on disability and abuse between 1989 and 1992, to investigate some of these issues and their findings are reported in *Child Abuse Review*, (Vol. 1, No. 3, 1992) They were told by one Social Services Team Leader: 'We accept that physical means of control are more acceptable for children with learning difficulties than for other children. Children are locked in their bedrooms at night. I know a child who is tied to a chair to keep him safe. We accept the differences – but should we?'

A range of abusive practices were uncovered in the study. These included force feeding; photographing (in a medical context) children's impairments in intrusive, insensitive ways; medical rehabilitation programmes which are experienced as painful and oppressive; physical restraint; misuse of medication; depriving of visitors; opening letters; listening to telephone calls; open days where strangers intrude on children's privacy; withdrawal of privileges; financial and property abuse.

By broadening the definition of abuse, disabled adults challenge us to consider a huge range of experiences that many non-disabled children would not have to suffer. The discrimination, segregation and disadvantage that disabled children experience as part of their daily lives could itself be construed as abusive (and many believe it is). The use of language regarding disability in itself tells disabled people that they are not valued and some have described this experience of discrimination, of rejection, as emotional abuse, and so it is important to acknowledge it as such.

I have been criticised for including these experiences within the framework of child protection/abuse on the grounds of 'muddying the waters'. Whether we call these things 'abuse', 'abusive practices', 'infringements of children's rights' or 'system abuse', allowing such practices to continue means that disabled children are harmed and their basic human rights infringed.

Disabled people have only just started to give voice to their experience of physical and emotional abuse. There are still very few opportunities for them to express their experience of sexual abuse but – if these opportunities are created – we should expect challenges to official definitions and perceptions of sexual abuse similar to the questioning of definitions of physical and emotional abuse.

In the case of sexual abuse the most common definition given is that attributed to Kempe and Kempe.

> The involvement of developmentally immature children and adolescents in sexual activities which they cannot fully comprehend, to which they cannot give informed consent and which violate the taboo of social rules (quoted in Kempe and Kempe, 1984, p. 9).

This definition has been criticised by feminists for not including the idea that force or the threat of force, may be used, and that adults' power over the child may constitute sufficient coercive power. (Ash 1984 quoted in MacLeod and Saraga, 1988 p. 19.) Moreover, the definition does not say anything about the abuser. Indeed, it describes the child.

What do we know about disabled children's experience of sexual abuse?

In fact we know very little about disabled children's experience of sexual abuse. There is very little statistical information.

Social services authorities are required to keep registers of all the children in their area who have been reported as abused or who are considered to be at risk. By the year ending March 1993 there were 32,500 names on the child protection registers for England and 63 per cent of girls on the Register were registered under sexual abuse (Department of Health, Press Release, 21 April 1994). What was not noted or documented was whether any of these children had impairments. Such notification is not required and has never been collected.

There is virtually no research on abuse of disabled children in the UK, although work by Hilary Brown and Vicky Turk of Canterbury University explores the abuse of learning disabled adults (Brown and Turk, 1992) and the most recent study of sexual abuse experienced by 1,244 16–21 year olds include a small sample of disabled young people (Kelly, Regan and Burton, 1991).

TABLE 1:
Multiple Abuse Experiences by Gender for Disabled Respondents

	Women		Men	
	No.	%	No.	%
No experiences	8	28	16	62
One experience	10	34	2	8
Two experiences	4	14	3	12
Three experiences	5	17	1	4
Four experiences	-	-	-	-
Five experiences	2	7	-	-
% Reporting Abuse		72		32
	Base of 29 women and 26 men			

Source: Kelly, Regan and Burton, 1991

The main findings of this research overall suggested that one in two girls and one in four boys experience some form of sexual abuse before their eighteenth birthday. For disabled children the study would seem to suggest that the prevalence rates are two out of three girls, and one out of every three boys. However, we have to be careful about generalising from such a small sample.

Attempts to measure the incidence of sexual abuse of disabled children have been made by American and Canadian researchers. However, compared to the research on non-disabled children it is inadequate and sparse. Westcott and Cross (1995) provide a detailed review of the research concerning abuse of disabled children, which includes the following (Table 2).

TABLE 2:
Sexual Abuse of Disabled Children

STUDY	CHILDREN	SOURCE OF INFORMATION	FINDINGS
Welbourne *et al.*, 1983 (US)	39 women blind from birth or prior to age of 10 years	Interviews	Over 50% women experienced at least one incident of forced sexual contact.
Chamberlain *et al.*, 1984 (US)	87 young women having learning difficulties to differing degrees	Records and Interviews with young women	1. 25% of young women had been sexually abused, narrowly defined as 'attempted or successful coerced intercourse'. 2. Mean age at time of abuse 14 years.
Doucette, 1986 (US)	30 disabled and 32 non-disabled women	Self-reports of childhood experiences	1. 47% of disabled women sexually abused, compared to 34% non-disabled women. 2. Increased risk [of abuse].
Sullivan *et al.*, 1987 (US)	1. All members of 9th grade at residential school for deaf children. 2. 150 pupils at residential school for deaf children. 3. 322 students at further education college for hearing Impaired students. 4. 100 deaf children attending either residential or mainstream schools	1. Questionnaire survey. 2. Individual interviews. 3. Questionnaire survey. 4. Individual interviews.	1. 50% children reported sexual abuse. 2. 50% children reported sexual abuse. 3. 13 students (4%) reported sexual abuse and 24 students (7%) reported both sexual and physical abuse. 4. Of 64 children attending residential schools, 40 (63%) sexually abused at school, 10 (16%) sexually abused at home, and 15 (23%) sexually abused at both school and home. Of 35 children in mainstream schools, 21 (60%) sexually abused at home, 9 (26%) sexually abused at school, and 5 (14%) sexually abused at both home and school.

TABLE 2: (contd)

STUDY	CHILDREN	SOURCE OF INFORMATION	FINDINGS
Ammerman *et al.*, 1989 (US)	148 children aged 3-19 years, psychiatrically referred and having multiple impairments of varying severity	Medical, psychiatric, nursing and social-work records	1. 39% of children showed evidence of past or current abuse (19% definite, 20% probable/possible). 2. Of these 39%, 36% were sexually abused. 3. Increased risk [of abuse].
Hard (cited in Mayer & Brenner, 1989), (US)	95 learning disabled adults	Not known	1. Over 50% returns reported abuse. 2. 70 children were suspected victims of sexual abuse, and 50 children were confirmed sexually abused.
Kennedy, 1989 (UK)	Deaf children known to professionals	Survey of 156 teachers and social workers for the deaf	1. 83% females and 32% males had been sexually abused. 2. In 45% cases, this was prior to victim's 18th birthday.
Benedict *et al.*, 1990 (US)	500 children with multiple physical and learning impairments	Medical, nursing, social-work and clinical records	1. Reports of abuse and neglect filed in 10.6% cases. 2. Of these 10.6%, 8.8% were sexually abused. 3. No increased risk [of abuse].
Sinason (undated) (UK)	40 children with learning impairments and emotional problems referred to Tavistock clinic 1991-92	Psychotherapist seeing children	1. 30 (75%) had been sexually abused. 2. Of 30, 21 (70%) were girls and 9 (33%) were boys.

Source: Westcott and Cross (1995)

Given the increased attention paid to sexual abuse of non-disabled children by researchers and child care professionals in recent years, we need to look at why this work has not included disabled children.

Barriers to knowledge of sexual abuse of disabled children

The practices and assumptions of both researchers and child care professionals can make it unlikely that sexual abuse of disabled children will be recognised or information gathered about their experiences.

Research methods

Research models in themselves can create barriers to recognition and the gathering of information. Most research methods presume the respondent to have no physical or

sensory impairments or learning difficulties. The questionnaires used by researchers in this field require sight, motor
control in order to fill in the questionnaire, relatively high
levels of comprehension and concentration. Similarly audio
taped interviews require speech.

Researchers rarely consider the need for self-completion
questionnaires to be in formats suitable for blind children or
adults, or for people with learning difficulties, or how those
with significant physical impairments can be helped to
complete a questionnaire in confidence. Face to face interviews do not address the needs of children and adults with
communication impairments, learning difficulties or those
who use sign language. Children whose first language is not
English will experience additional barriers to being represented within any research about abuse: few research projects
incorporate the costs of Sign Language Interpreters or other
minority language interpreters.

Above all, researchers often feel threatened and deskilled
when faced with the prospect of including disabled children in
their studies; the barriers feel too great.

Assumptions about sexual abuse and disabled children

Until recently, a common assumption held by both researchers
and those working in child protection was that impairment
protected children from abuse. There was the belief that
adults in society would either not find disabled children
attractive (sic) or would feel sorry for them (Marchant 1991,
pp. 22–4). They simply would not be targeted for any form of
sexual activity. After all, so it was believed, even disabled
adults should not/would not engage in sexual activity, in
which case sexually abusing a disabled child was certainly not
likely. This has diverted attention away from protecting
disabled children.

Even when the possibility of sexual abuse is recognised,
those working in child protection often fail to see disabled
children as part of their main body of work and concern. A
policy maker in the field of child protection, on being asked
what measures were taken to safeguard disabled children,
replied 'Let me sort out the normal child first' (Kennedy and

Kelly, 1992, pp. 147–9). There is also evidence of a belief that abuse experienced by disabled children is somehow of less significance than that experienced by non-disabled children. This kind of attitude was reflected in one counsellor's comment to a mother whose disabled son had been sexually abused: 'At least it didn't happen to one of your non-disabled children' (Marchant, personal communication).

The BASPCAN Disability and Abuse Working Party heard evidence of indicators of abuse being interpreted as associated with the child's impairment. For example, one General Practitioner said to a child's mother, 'Didn't you know, Mrs Jones, that deaf children masturbate because they are frustrated about their communication?' A paediatrician, on examining a child with hypotonic spastic quadriplegia who had vaginal injuries, anal scars and a sexually transmitted disease, stated that 'These symptoms could be due to an obscure syndrome'.

Children who have been abused blame themselves. This is so for non-disabled and disabled children. Abusers manipulate children so that they feel this way and therefore will not tell. What is different for non-disabled and disabled children is the response to them when and if they disclose. If adults believe – as they often do – that no one would harm a disabled child and that they are not 'attractive', disclosure of abuse can be met with a belief that the child must surely have 'got it wrong'. This is particularly so in the case of children with learning difficulties. If disabled children should 'tell' in other ways, by behavioural signs and indications, for example, anger, regression, soiling, wetting or fears, these are often attributed to their distress about their impairment or their experience of disability.

Barriers to disclosure
Particular features of some disabled children's lives need to be recognised as barriers to the disclosure and recognition of abuse. One important factor is the physical dependence that some children have on their abusers. To be dependent on an adult for personal care needs, for regular medical attention (such as injections) or physiotherapy, places a child (or indeed

an adult) in a potentially vulnerable situation. The BASPCAN Working Party were told of one child who expressed fear at telling the social worker what had happened in case her family heard about the abuse and also told of being threatened with being sent back to hospital if anyone found out.

Children in such situations will find it very difficult to disclose abuse as they will fear that their basic needs will no longer be met. Their fear may also include worries about who would replace their abusive carer. Some children's physical dependence is such that they fear for their lives.

Programmes aimed at preventing child abuse teach children to say no to things they do not like, particularly touch, and then to get away, to find someone they trust and to tell (the 'No, Go, Tell' principle). For non-disabled children such advice is useful and has sometimes been used to good effect, but for disabled children these principles do not take account of their impairments. Many may use non-verbal forms of communication. To say 'no' to an abuser may be very difficult and to tell someone even more so. This is compounded by the fact that many forms of augmentative communication systems, particularly symbol systems, using finger or eye pointing on boards, censor all use of words/symbols to describe genitals or sexual acts. Children who use symbol boards by finger or eye pointing may only be understood by one or two key people in their lives – and what if one of these people is the abuser?

Children who do not use speech will often find that child protection teams are not skilled in their particular communication system. It will not always be possible, therefore, for the child to find someone who will understand what they are saying. However, telling is only a start, being believed by the adult is also a barrier to be addressed. The myth that impairment 'protects' a child from abuse leads adults to disbelieve children's attempts to tell their experiences. And a disabled child – particularly one who is in some form of segregated provision – may find it very difficult to 'go', to get away from the abuser.

Moreover, the disabled child may also be so lacking in confidence and self-esteem that a vicious circle is set up in which the child is never able to disclose that they are being abused. Indeed, a disabled child's general experience of abusive practices may make it difficult even to name something as sexual abuse. The BASPCAN Working Party received evidence from a disabled adult which illustrates this.

> It did not seem anything out of the ordinary. The way the porter looked inside my nightie and lifted it up and touched me seemed, I think, just like what had been done to me a thousand times before by doctors and other people who wanted to look and prod and poke and talk – all as though I did not exist. All my early hospital experiences 'groomed' me for abuse. If you have never been given the opportunity to object to a doctor taking off your clothes just to look at your leg or if you objected to a doctor pulling down your knickers just to measure your leg but the doctor carried on regardless then how do you recognise that what a porter does to you in a lift is called sexual abuse and that you could/should say no. It all seemed the same to me.

Are disabled children 'vulnerable' to sexual abuse?

When it *is* recognised that disabled children are vulnerable to abuse some researchers and practitioners are in danger of focusing on the impairment and the child rather than on the abuser and society. Some researchers tend to see impairment as an 'abuse provoking characteristic'. For example, Krents *et al.* state that '. . . children who are victims of abuse often have qualities that make them different or difficult to care for. These include mental and physical disabilities as well as behavioural and emotional problems' (Krents *et al.*, 1987, p. 80)

Ammerman *et al.* (1989) use descriptions of disabled abused children which are value-laden and decidedly negative and blaming. They describe 'behavioural disturbances' that are 'aversive to parents', 'maladaptive responses', 'inappropriate vocalisation' and parents who have 'an inability to control a child's deviant behaviour' (quoted in Kelly 1992, p. 160). Feminist theory challenges these arguments by pointing out that, apart from the obvious point that children react to abuse and that their behaviour is a consequence rather than a cause of their maltreatment, these theoretical positions focus on the child rather than on the abusing adult when explaining why abuse occurs (Kelly, 1992).

If we accept that disabled children are at a particular risk of abuse – and they do seem to be – we have to look at the social world in which they live in order to understand this. In other words, we need to look at how such vulnerability is *created*. Two particular factors can be identified as important.

Disabling attitudes

Negative social values placed on children who have impairments give both the children and potential abusers strong messages.

In the course of her research on the development of deaf children, Susan Gregory interviewed parents and their hearing-impaired children. Two parents who had deaf children following Rubella in pregnancy expressed themselves as follows:

> 'I had Rubella, I should have had an abortion.'
> 'I am a great believer in it [abortion]. Even now sex is casual, every baby should be wanted, so erase it if it is not. I wouldn't have brought it into the world to be like she is. Don't bring someone into the world if you know you've had German measles, honestly. Thank God you don't get many deaf kids.'

Both the young people were aware of their parent's feelings:

> 'Mother told me she would have aborted me if she had known about German measles.'
> Susan Gregory: 'What do you feel about that?'
> 'Yes, I agree about handicapped being aborted.'
> Susan Gregory: 'Deaf as well?'
> 'Yes.'

A general attitude that children with physical or sensory impairments, or learning difficulties, should not have been born at all forms an important part of the vulnerability to abuse experienced by disabled children. If children are seen as 'inferior', 'worth-less' this may be taken by offenders as permission to abuse. Children themselves will internalise the idea that they are 'defective' and impossibly far from achieving acceptability. The kind of messages that disabled children receive about their value are summed up by the comment of one young man with cerebral palsy who had experienced sexual abuse. He said, 'Why bugger up a normal child, I was defective already.'

This powerlessness can also be created and reinforced by the way that disabled children are often over-protected, discouraged from thinking things out for themselves and not allowed to make choices. The resulting passivity will make it harder for a child to trust their own instincts about what is acceptable behaviour from the abusive adult, and to seek out an adult who might protect them.

Segregation creates vulnerability to abuse

Research suggests that the risk of being sexually abused within an institutional setting is two to four times as high as of being sexually abused in the community. (Rindfleisch and Rabb, 1984; Shaughnessy, 1984). There are particular factors associated with residential care which create a vulnerability to abuse. Isolation from the wider society – which may be created by geographical location and/or inadequate links with family and community – can make disclosure impossible. Increased numbers of adult care-givers in a residential, as compared to a family, setting will increase the possibility of one being an abuser. Indeed, offenders may think it is safer to abuse children in a residential setting and may 'target' such vulnerable groups. Segregated provision also gives disabled children messages about themselves which can result in low self-esteem. As Theresia Degener, a lawyer representing survivors of abuse and who is herself disabled, says,

Children who grow up in an institution or who receive segregated education in a special school for the disabled learn that they are abnormal and should not be the way they are. This is the reason why they receive all kinds of therapy, spend a significant proportion of their childhood in hospital, and go more often to the doctor than their non-disabled peers. (Degener, 1992, p. 152)

Within segregated education, disabled children are given little information on safety and prevention programmes and are less likely than non-disabled children to receive sex education. At a recent training course I ran for teachers of deaf children from six schools or units in one local authority area, not one was implementing a safety and prevention programme for their pupils.

Responses to disabled children's experience of sexual abuse

Unfortunately even when sexual abuse experienced by a disabled child has been disclosed and recognised, responses can still be discriminatory and disempowering.

Child protection workers can feel overwhelmed when a disabled child discloses abuse in that the practical problems of investigating the claim and giving the child support appear insurmountable. The experience of Ruth Marchant and Marcus Page in trying to facilitate appropriate help for a group of abused children with multiple impairments in a large

TABLE 3

COMMENTS	REFRAMED
The child is the problem	**The facility/worker is the problem**
'He can't get into the building'	'Our building is not accessible'
'She can't get into the therapy room'	'Our therapy rooms are poorly located'
'He can't use our toilets'	'Our toilet facilities are inadequate'
'He can't talk'	'We don't know how to communicate using Bliss/Makaton/Rebus or Sign Language'
'She wouldn't have the understanding to cope with counselling'	'We do not have the commitment, time, knowledge or confidence to work with disabled children'
'He doesn't have the language skills to cope with group work'	ditto

Source: Marchant and Page, 1992, p. 31

residential establishment illustrates the way that practical issues can be presented as barriers. They discovered that the reasons given for not being able to offer help to the children were diverse but all tended to focus on the child as the problem rather than the barriers posed by the physical environment and lack of appropriate support or skills. Marchant and Page listed the workers' comments and then reframed them in a way that avoids seeing the child as the problem, as illustrated in Table 3. Marchant and Page's 'reframing' illustrates that the onus has usually been placed on the disabled child to fit the programme available, rather than vice versa, and that this effectively 'blames' the child for unsuitable or inaccessible provision.

A feeling of being overwhelmed by both practical problems and 'complicating factors' may be particularly common where ethnic minority children are concerned, or children who have significant communication difficulties, or 'challenging behaviour'. Such a reaction will merely confirm children's feelings of rejection whereas what they need is an affirmation of their worth, and help in sorting out how they have been disempowered by discriminatory attitudes. As Droisen writes, 'In the end it can become impossible to unravel whether your feelings are due to the abuse, or the racism . . . They merge and intensify each other; for survival they need to be unravelled' (Droisen, 1989, quoted in *The ABCD Pack*, p. 36).

It is important to understand the traumatic, additional effect the lack of service provision has on the disabled abused child who may already believe 'I was abused because I am disabled' or 'I am not a valuable and worthwhile person'. These beliefs could be confirmed when it becomes apparent that no one is willing or able to offer them suitable help and support. Disabled children generally are devalued by today's society and, by failing to tailor child protection services to their needs, this message is further compounded for the child in need of protection and help in the face of abuse.

However, it is potentially equally damaging to insist that disabled children are children first and foremost and that methods of working with non-disabled children are just as appropriate. Taking the 'children first' position means that the reality of impairment – and the needs associated with it – can be denied. This position also does not challenge the oppression associated with the disabling experience of others' reactions to impairment. Disabled children are not children who just happen to have a physical or sensory impairment, or a learning difficulty; this denies the reality of the needs arising from impairment, making it more difficult to recognise that these children do require different techniques for disclosure and response to be successful. For example, a child with cerebral palsy may need a thicker pen so that she can hold it to write; a blind child can use shapes rather than colours to express feelings; a deaf child needs a Sign Language Interpreter.

Moreover, disabled children quite quickly establish for themselves the connection between disability and abuse. They may not articulate it within a framework of discrimination, oppression or prejudice but they may more concretely describe the practicalities of their situation: 'I didn't see him coming' (blind child); 'I didn't hear him coming' (deaf child); 'I could not get away' (mobility impaired); 'I could not tell' (child using other forms of communication such as British Sign Language, Makaton, Blissymbolics, Rebus). Helping such children to understand that abuse happened because someone chose to abuse them and that the abusers may have used their very impairment to gain advantage is a painful and distressing task.

Many therapists will try to argue that the impairment had no bearing on the abuse happening since 'many non-disabled children are abused also' but this completely denies the internal gut feelings of the older child who does understand society's values and declares 'I was abused because I was disabled'. During my work with disabled children over the last five years they have said things like, 'I was abused because they saw me as useless'; 'I was abused because everyone thinks I'm useless'; 'I was abused because everyone thinks I'm useless and not valuable'; 'I was abused because they knew I couldn't tell'; 'I was abused because they never liked me or wanted me'; 'I was abused because I was already defective'.

'The 'Children First' principle simply does not allow the child protection worker to understand the additional needs of disabled children. It is a principle which means that additional resources do not have to be found, for service providers can usefully argue that whatever they already do for non-disabled abused children will be suitable for disabled children. The reality is felt not at managerial level but at ground level where well-meaning and caring workers face the fact that working with a disabled child who has been abused is more complex and that they have never been trained to deal with the situations that might arise out of this. They ask questions such as: 'How do I help a non-verbal child express all their feelings?' 'How do I work with a child who is visually impaired when most of my work involves drawing and painting?'; 'How do I help a child with cerebral palsy who does not use speech or arms or hands to express their anger?' or 'How do I work with a deaf child using British Sign Language using an interpreter?'

Child protection workers also have to address the difficult question of how disabled childen can be helped with the painful knowledge that their abuser may well have targeted them because of their impairment.

Unfortunately, professionals' focus on impairment tends to to take place within a medical model framework, with the result that abused children and adults are conceptualised as victims and as 'ill'. The result of this can be that the self-image of those who have been abused has been further undermined. It also becomes more difficult to recognise the factors outside the child which are responsible for the abuse. In other words, instead of focusing on the perpetrator and the disempowering experience of a disabling society it is easy to slip into focusing on the perceived inadequacies of the child.

For these reasons, many adults who have been sexually abused have rejected the medical model and 'victim' labels and opted for the positive use of the word 'survivors'. This acknowledges their strategies for coping and their strength in the face of their adversity. Increasingly, survivors look for support and help from fellow survivors, counsellors and friends. The abuse survivor views their condition as a result of life events and not a medical or psychiatric illness. The survivor may feel that s/he needs to develop strength and power rather than become 'well' or 'better', making empowerment rather than recovery their goal.

Issues for the future

While there is now more recognition of disabled children's experience of abuse, there is a need to be clearer about the way children with physical, sensory and/or intellectual impairments are disabled by the society in which they live and how this makes them vulnerable to abuse – sexual, emotional and physical. Vulnerable children are created by society's stereotypes, negative attitudes, expectations and prognosis and by prejudice and disablism. It is not the impairment itself that places these children at risk but adults' responses to that impairment.

We would all be helped in this task by a greater knowledge of the experience of abuse from disabled children's points of view. As Liz Kelly writes,

> Of particular concern is how few of the studies . . . [of sexual abuse of disabled children] are based on direct contact with children/young people/adults with disabilities. What we think we know is based primarily on clinicians', practitioners' and parents' perceptions – the vast majority of whom . . . are able-bodied. Nor is there much evidence of an awareness of the additional factors of race, class, gender and sexuality. (Kelly, 1992, p. 165)

We need research which is based on the direct experience of disabled adults and children; in particular we need to make it possible for adult survivors to come together to articulate and share their experiences and for child protection workers to learn from these experiences about the best ways of preventing sexual abuse of disabled children.

Paying serious attention to children's and adults' communication needs is an important part of making disclosure and survival work possible. Effective communication is necessary in order to: carry out safety programmes in both mainstream and 'special' schools; assess children who are thought to have been abused; enable the child to express his/her wishes and feelings; enable the child to have his/her experience understood by child protection workers and the legal system; enable the child to have therapy or counselling.

Feminist child protection workers must continue to acquire knowledge and understanding about disabled children who are abused and must transform the established negative stereotypes within the child protection field. This can only be done by building alliances with disabled people and enabling their experiences to be recognised.

References
ABCD Consortium (1994) *The ABCD Pack: Abuse and children who are disabled*, ABCD Consortium (c/o NSPCC Child Protection Training Group).

Ammerman, R. *et al.* (1989) 'Abuse and neglect in psychiatrically hospitalised multi-handicapped children', *Child Abuse and Neglect*, Vol. 13, No. 3, pp. 335–44.

Ash, Angie (1984) *Father-Daughter Sexual Abuse: The abuse of paternal authority*, University College of North Wales.

Brown, Hilary and Turk, Vicky (1992) 'Defining sexual abuse as it affects adults with learning disabilities', in *Mental Handicap*, 20, pp. 44–5.

Cameron, D. and Frazer, E. (1987) *The Lust to Kill*, Polity Press.

Chamberlain, A. *et al.* (1984) 'Issues in fertility control for mentally retarded female adolescents: 1. Sexual activity, sexual abuse, and contraception', in *Paediatrics*, 73, pp. 445–50.

Degener, Theresia (1992) 'The right to be different: Implications for child protection', in *Child Abuse Review*, Vol. 1, No. 3, pp. 151–6.

Doucette, J. (1986) *Violent Acts Against Disabled Women*, DAWN Canada.

Droisen, A. and Driver, E., eds., (1989) *Child Sexual Abuse: Feminist perspectives*, Macmillan.

Gregory, Susan (1994) 'The developing deaf child', in Laurenzi, C. and Hindley, P., eds., *Keep Deaf Children in Mind: Current issues in mental health*, National Deaf Children's Society.

Kelly, Liz (1988) *Surviving Sexual Violence*, Polity Press.

Kelly, Liz (1992) 'Case Study II: Can't hear or won't hear? The evidential experience of children with disabilities', in *Child Abuse Review*, Vol, 1, No. 3, 188–90.

Kelly, Liz, Regan, Linda and Burton, Sheila (1991) *An Exploratory Study of Sexual Abuse in a Sample of 16–21 year olds*, University of North London.

Kempe, R. and Kempe, C. (1984) *The Common Secret*, Freeman, New York.

Kennedy, Margaret (1989) 'The abuse of deaf children', in *Child Abuse Review*, Vol. 3, No. 1, pp. 3–7.

Kennedy, Margaret (1992) 'Case Study I: Children with severe disabilities: Too many assumptions', in *Child Abuse Review*, Vol. 1, No. 3, pp. 185–7.

Kennedy, Margaret (1994) 'Confusion of signs and indicators', in ABCD Consortium, *The ABCD Pack: Abuse and children who are disabled*, ABCD Consortium (c/o NSPCC Child Protection Training Group), pp. 83–7.

Kennedy, Margaret and Kelly, Liz (1992) 'Inclusion not exclusion', in *Child Abuse Review*, Vol. 1, No. 3, pp. 147–9.

Krents, E., Schulman, V. and Brenner, S. (1987) 'Child abuse and the disabled child: perspectives for parents', in *Volta Review*, Vol. 89, No. 5, pp. 78–95.

MacLeod, Mary and Saraga, Esther (1988) 'Challenging the orthodoxy: towards a feminist theory and practice', in *Feminist Review*, No. 28, pp. 16–55.

Marchant, Ruth (1991) 'Myths and facts about sexual abuse and children with disabilities', in *Child Abuse Review*, Vol. 5, No. 2, pp. 22–4.

Nelson, Sarah (1987) *Incest: Fact and Myth*, Stramullion.

Rindfleisch, N. and Rabb, J. (1984) 'How much of a problem is resident mistreatment in child welfare institutions?' in *Child Abuse and Neglect*, 8, pp. 33–40.

Russell, Diana (1986) *The Secret Trauma*, Basic Books, New York.

Shaughnessy, M. F. (1984) 'Institutional child abuse', in *Children and Youth Services Review*, 6, pp. 311–18.

Sinason, V. (undated) Untitled paper, Tavistock and Portman Clinics Special Committee.

Sullivan, P. M. *et al.* (1992) 'The effects of psychotherapy on behaviour problems of sexually abused deaf children', in *Child Abuse and Neglect*, 16, pp. 297–307.

Westcott, Helen and Cross, Merry (1995) *This Far and No Further: Towards ending the abuse of disabled children*, Venture Press.

CHAPTER SIX

POWER IN THE HOUSE:
Women with Learning Difficulties Organising Against Abuse
The Powerhouse

The Powerhouse is a group of disabled (mainly women with learning difficulties) and non-disabled women who have shared with each other their experiences of emotional, physical, sexual and verbal abuse and who campaigned for a refuge – a safe place – especially for women with learning difficulties. This is their story of what they did.

Some years ago, women with learning difficulties at a Community College in East London started meeting together. One of the things they talked about was the way women with learning difficulties are often hurt by things other people do and say to them. Some of the things they said about the abuse experienced by women with learning difficulties were:

'Women with learning difficulties feel terrible and confused about what they should do if they are abused, where they can go for help.'

'Women feel lost, frightened and stuck.'

'Women feel squashed, there ain't no places for women to go.'

'Why is women getting attacked? Why is it always women?'

'Why is men doing these things to women? It's dangerous to women and children.'

'Some women are too scared to get out of the house, to get out in the dark, the men follow you, I don't trust them.'

'Women get beaten up in their homes, in their hostels, or they set fire to their house or whatever.'

The women with learning difficulties in the group felt that the refuges that there were for women weren't right for them and that the women who organised the refuges hadn't thought about women with learning difficulties. One of the women, Alison Hazel, wrote a poem which said,

> Why don't you think of this?
> You've made it for non-disabled women,
> you've built for non-disabled women.
> You should always think of making for Disabled
>   women too.
> We can do the same things as you can do too.
> Don't think if you have Learning Difficulty you can't
>   do anything.
> We have the right to do the same things as you too.
> It is true.

The women with learning difficulties said,

> If we could say what we really want, it would be a safe house, just for women with learning difficulties, with women workers, women counsellors, at a confidential address, where we could stay for a while and get strong by being able to talk about our experiences and learning to do more things for ourselves.

The women decided to meet to talk about this and asked other women to join. Since the beginning of 1991 the group has been meeting every week. It includes women with learning difficulties, disabled women, Black and white women and lesbians. The group called itself Powerhouse and wrote a song (to the tune of *Oh, When the Saints Go Marching in* . . .)

> We have the right
> to live our lives
> we have the right to live our lives.
>
> For we are proud Disabled Women,
> we have the right to live our lives.
>
> There's shelter in
> the Powerhouse
> there's shelter in the Powerhouse.
>
> For we are proud Disabled Women,
> we have the right to live our lives.

Ways of working together

We needed a number of things so that we could carry on meeting: a safe place to meet; transport and support to get to the meetings; support at the meetings; advice. We also needed to have fun at the meetings so that we wanted to keep coming to them.

We had to change how we talk and how we do things so that everyone is involved as much as possible and understands what is happening. We want to make sure that women with learning difficulties can work with women without learning difficulties and that women with learning difficulties will lead the project.

These are the rules that we have for our meetings:

Talk in short sentences and short words;
Use drawings;
Respect what people say;
Respect different women;
Listen in meetings;
Take responsibility: say if you don't understand
        give your ideas
        say if you don't agree.

Getting started

In order to get money from social services and from other

funders we had to register as a charity and draw up rules about what the group is for and how it works. This all took a lot of time and was very difficult to do sometimes because the way other people work doesn't allow for the way women with learning difficulties need to do things.

We started working with East London Housing Association. They got money from the Housing Corporation to build a safe house for us. We worked with them to find the land and design the house. We asked the architects to make the plans easy for us to understand and we looked at all the things that needed to be done to make the house possible for women with all kinds of needs to live there. We wanted the house to be right for women who use wheelchairs and for women who can't see and/or can't hear.

We met with the architects and people from the Housing Association many times to talk about what the house should be like. We decided that the Housing Association should manage the house and the support workers but the Powerhouse rules say that women with learning difficulties will always be the largest group on the Management Committee and that there must also be women with physical impairments, Black women and lesbians.

Because there was so much going on the Powerhouse decided to set up three smaller groups who would work on: the house, money and policy, employment.

The housing group was involved in the design of the house and all the small but important choices like colours, carpets, furniture. The safe house has six flats with two bedrooms, a lounge and a kitchen in each. There is also a room which can be used as a meeting or dining room by everyone who lives there, a room for counselling, an office, staff sleep-in room, laundry and a project room.

The money group worked on getting grants and donations so that we could employ a Fundraiser/Finance Worker and a Development Worker, and buy office equipment. To give a good service to women in the refuge will cost about £375,000 per year. A lot of this will come from the health and social services authorities which refer women to the safe house but we will also need to raise money from charities and trusts, companies and through fund-raising events.

The policy group worked on how we should go about recruiting and employing two workers, how the Management Committee should work, and deciding what we needed to work on so that we can set up the house and support. The group is also raising people's awareness about the abuse experienced by women with learning difficulties and what investigators and the courts need to do to make it possible for the abuse to stop. Once the house is opened the policy group will look at how we record what is happening, what is going well and what isn't.

When the house was half-built we started to plan sending out information about it to health and social service authorities. We had to decide on a name for the house and we chose the Beverley Lewis House. Beverley Lewis was a Black deaf-blind woman with learning difficulties who had a warm personality and a lot to offer. At the age of 23 she died, wrapped in newspapers and weighing less than five stone. She had been a great joy to her family but her mother had a lot of mental health difficulties and was not able to give Beverley the support she needed. Although her family asked a lot of times for help from health and social services they didn't get the help they needed. Beverley Lewis died because the welfare system didn't protect her as an important human being.

With the support of Beverley Lewis' family Powerhouse have named the safe house after her so that her memory lives on.

Women with learning difficulties are often not given the chance to live independently; they often have the kind of experience which one woman involved in Powerhouse has written a poem about:

This is my home.
Staff wear uniforms.
This is my home.
No money of our own.
This is my home.
No choice of food.

This is my home.
I'm not allowed in my kitchen.
This is my home.
Why can't I choose what food I eat?
This is my home.
Why can't I spend my money on what I want?
This is my home.
Why can't I have a key?
This is my home.
I want to lock my bathroom door.
This is my home.
People come into my bedroom without asking.
This is my home.
The staff don't let us have our own things.
This is my home.
The staff have no respect for us.
This is my home.
Why can't we go out when we want to.
Is this my home?

The Beverley Lewis House will give women the chance to get away from abuse and also to live independently with whatever support they might need. Our leaflet tells women how the House will help them (see pp. 141–2).

Although the Beverley Lewis House is in London, women with learning difficulties from any part of the country can come to it. Women will be treated with respect and helped to make choices for themselves. They will be able to stay for up to two years and helped to move on to a home of their own.

This is the first and only refuge like this. The women involved in Powerhouse want to make sure that it works well and that more and more is done to stop women with learning difficulties being abused.

The Beverley Lewis House is a Safe House

for Women with Learning Difficulties who feel frightened, or are being treated in a bad way

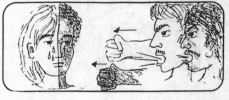

and want it to stop.

If you are being or have been attacked or treated in a bad way

you can do something about it.

You can telephone the Beverley Lewis House

or you could ask a friend to telephone for you.

A woman worker will listen to you on the phone

and can arrange to meet you about living in the Safe House, if you want,

until you find your own <u>safe</u> home.

If you come and live in the Safe House

you will live with other women
who have also been attacked, or who
have been treated in a bad way.

You can be on your own when you want to.

There will be women workers who can help you learn to do more things
<u>for yourself</u>, like:

* Cooking, using
  kitchen things

* Going shopping

* Travelling

* Choosing your
  own clothes

* Using money

* Speaking up
  for yourself

If you have a child or children
they can also come with you.

There will be a woman counsellor who
you can talk to about your problems.

The Beverley Lewis House is fully accessible

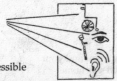

CHAPTER SEVEN

PRENATAL TESTING AND THE PREVENTION OF IMPAIRMENT: *A Woman's Right to Choose*?

Ruth Bailey

This chapter considers the implications of prenatal testing for disabled people, particularly in the light of advances in genetic knowledge which are creating more possibilities for the prevention of impairments.

Women are now routinely offered one or more prenatal screening tests during pregnancy. These range from a simple blood test to discover the 'probability' of the woman's child having spina bifida or Down's syndrome, to the more invasive and risky amniocentesis, which draws fluid from the amniotic sac so that it can be analysed for indications of genetic impairment. If any test indicates that the potential child would have an impairment, the mother is offered an abortion.

Non-disabled feminists have broadly welcomed prenatal testing. They have viewed it as another means through which women can gain control over their own reproduction. However, from the mid-1980s, some feminist writers have also noted that this control comes at a price (see for example, Farrant, 1985; Hubbard, 1986; Oakley, 1986; Rothman, 1989). That price includes the anxiety which now dominates early pregnancy – deciding whether to undergo testing, awaiting results – and the difficult decision to be made about continuing the pregnancy or electing for abortion if an impairment is diagnosed.

Nonetheless, implicit support for prenatal testing was evident when non-disabled feminists used the general consensus which exists around abortion on\ the ground of impairment to strengthen their general case for resisting attempts to amend the 1967 Abortion Act. Support against amendments to this legislation was mobilised not only on grounds of a general defence of women's 'right to choose' but also in terms of defending the possibility of selective abortion when impairment has been diagnosed through prenatal testing.

More recently, prenatal testing has been discussed in the context of rapid expansion in knowledge about human genetics. The medical application of this knowledge means that many more impairments can now be diagnosed prenatally. The development of new methods of assisted reproduction, such as so called 'test tube babies', also means that there are ways of avoiding the birth of a disabled child. This has led some to ask to what lengths women should be allowed or encouraged to go to have 'a perfect child'? It has also raised the spectre of Nazi Germany, where the ideological quest for a 'pure and healthy race' led to the holocaust. There is still little recognition that this included the systematic killing of disabled people (see Morris, 1991, Chapter Two; Gallagher, 1990; Burleigh, 1994; Proctor, 1988).

Disabled people, particularly disabled women, have taken issue with the feminist defence of selective abortion and raised a number of concerns about the growing use of prenatal testing facilitated by the new genetics. In short, they see prenatal testing and selective abortion as being rooted in and perpetuating the oppression of disabled people (see Davis, 1985, 1987; Glasman, 1987, 1991; Finger, 1984; Hannaford, 1985; Morris, 1991, 1992; Saxton, 1984; Wilkie, 1987, 1989).

For example, Jenny Morris argues that prejudice lies at the heart of the assumption that impairment is grounds enough for abortion. This assumption suggests that life for a disabled person is not worth living, and no one, she argues, should have the right to judge that another's quality of life would be so poor as to be not worth living. To allow abortion on the basis of such judgement is highly questionable in itself. In addition, she argues that because prenatal testing assumes that life for a disabled person is not worth living, it devalues all disabled people. Some also fear this approach to 'the problem' of impairment could deflect attention from the political demands of disabled people. Thus, Ellen Wilkie wrote

> As long as abortion continues to be permitted on grounds of disability, the future looks bleak as regards improving the lives of [disabled people] in all areas, e.g. access to buildings, employment, education and suitable housing. (Wilkie, 1989, p. 126)

I agree with the substance of disabled people's arguments. However, as a disabled feminist trying to understand prenatal testing as a social policy, those arguments also provoke many questions for me. How does the prejudice which is at the heart of prenatal testing manifest itself – and why? Is it possible to conceive of prenatal testing that does not use quality of life judgements? What political and social dynamics link the status of disabled people and prenatal testing?

My purpose in this chapter is to begin to explore these questions. I will do this by examining the medical and scientific context in which prenatal testing has been developed and is applied. I will then examine the social policies which govern the use of prenatal testing. In doing this, I hope it will be possible to clarify the nature of the risk that prenatal diagnosis poses to disabled people, to understand the risks of the 'new eugenics', and to conclude by making recommendations which go some way to avoid them.

The medical context of prenatal testing

The medical profession plays a significant role in prenatal testing: it is responsible for the development of prenatal diagnostic technology, as well as for overseeing the process of prenatal screening. How then do the views and interests of the medical profession influence the practice of prenatal testing and the decisions taken by individual women?

Questions of ethics

Prenatal testing is rarely done so that a condition can be treated in either the mother or the foetus. However, it is considered to be right or ethical to offer prenatal testing because, it is argued, it can prevent suffering by enabling a woman to consider abortion if her foetus has an impairment. How then, have the medical profession considered what degrees or types of impairment lead to such a level of suffering that offering a woman an abortion is justified?

One clinical geneticist, Clarke, suggests that this vital question has seldom been explicitly tackled by the medical profession. In their defence, the medical profession say that it is up to parents to decide if abortion is justified. But Clarke points out that this ignores the role of the profession in deciding which impairments are tested for, and suggests that in fact tests are introduced because they become technically possible rather than because they have been proven to be needed or to be a 'good thing' (Clarke, 1993).

Recently, this question has been debated in the medical press, prompted by the 1990 Human Fertilisation and Embryology Act. This permitted abortion up to birth on grounds of 'serious handicap', with medical practitioners having the day to day responsibility of deciding what constitutes 'serious handicap'. It would seem that serious handicap is being narrowly defined as those conditions which are fatal at, or near, birth (Bennet, 1993; Green, 1993; Lilford and Thornton, 1993). Perhaps this is indicative of the medical profession's uncertainty about the morality of allowing abortion after 24 weeks, that is after the point when a foetus is capable of being born alive.

The other interesting point which has emerged from this debate in the medical press is that, where Down's syndrome or spina bifida are prenatally diagnosed, abortion is offered 'on the grounds of the psychological impact they would have on the mother' not in the interests of the foetus (Bennet, 1993, p. 929). That is, abortions carried out if these conditions are diagnosed are done so under Section One of the 1967 Abortion Act, which permits abortion if the risks to the mother of continuing with the pregnancy are greater than the risk of termination. This is the so-called 'social' clause. Presumably, 'psychological impact' includes the strains and restrictions associated with the social and economic consequences faced by women caring for disabled children, of which there is much evidence.

Taken together, these points illustrate that the notion of suffering used by the medical profession includes physical pain and distress intrinsic to a particular medical condition, but also the psychological impact and social reaction to that impairment for both the potential child and the mother. There is also some evidence that this notion of suffering is extended still further, to include the impact of impairment on society. For example, in its review of prenatal diagnostic services, the Royal College of Physicians advises that if the parents are 'able to accept a degree of handicap in a child', doctors should remind them of the long-term implications of having a disabled child, including 'the situation that may arise after their own deaths' (Royal College of Physicians, 1989, p. 50). This could be seen to imply that even if the parents want to care for the disabled child, society may not, and that parents should take that into account.

This use of an expanded notion of suffering sheds some light on why Down's syndrome is one of the two most common conditions for which prenatal testing is offered. People with Down's rarely suffer physical pain or distress as a result of their impairment. It would seem that insofar as prenatal testing for Down's syndrome is about preventing 'suffering', it is the social or psychological suffering of others that is being considered.

The general difficulty with the ethical question cast in these terms is that the social and economic dimensions of 'suffering' are obscured, and are tackled at a medical and individual level, rather than a political level. Individual women do have to make decisions based on the economic and social circumstances in which they find themselves rather than hoping for or anticipating social change. However, when the general social and economic context of disability informs clinical decisions and practices, the risk is that the perceived social problem or disability becomes medicalised, with very little public discussion as to whether that is an appropriate or acceptable policy choice.

Medical views of impairment and disability

If there is little explicit discussion of the ethical reasons for prenatal testing, does the way medical professionals think about disability and impairment influence prenatal testing?

Modern medicine focuses on the structure and functioning of the body, on disease processes, and on the means to cure or mitigate the effects of diseases. Impairment, by definition, is something that is wrong with those structures and functions. Difficulties arise, I would argue, because medical habit suggests that level of function is intrinsically linked to quality of life.

For example, a medical researcher, Dr Seller, considered the possibilities of assessing severity of spina bifida prenatally. To do this, she first tried to establish a correlation between degree of impairment and quality of life. Her survey of young people with spina bifida concluded their quality of life was 'grim' (Seller, 1990, p. 446). Her evidence for this was based solely on bodily functions: that is, number of people who were incontinent, who were paralysed and so on. There was no mention of how the young people felt about these limitations, or of factors – medical or social – which impeded or improved their quality of life. In contrast, educationalist Elizabeth Anderson's study of young people with spina bifida and cerebral palsy found that while they faced a number of limitations, it was clear that these arose from a complexity of social circumstances, and that there was no simple correlation between degree of impairment and social situation (Anderson, 1982).

A related difficulty is the tendency for the disease or impairment to become the focus of attention, almost to the exclusion of the person. In the case of prenatal testing, of course, the only fact known about the foetus is whether it has an impairment or not. Even so, little attempt seems to be made to discuss the implications of the particular impairment diagnosed or its impact on life choices. For example, in a leaflet given to mothers undergoing prenatal screening, the first and only reference to the effects of Down's syndrome is

Babies born with Down's syndrome . . . have a characteristic appearance, are mentally handicapped, and may also have other birth defects. (Wolfson Institute, n.d.)

Moreover, the leaflet talks about diagnosing the conditions in the abstract, rather than diagnosing them in a foetus which is part of a mother. The implication is that, like a disease, these conditions can be 'removed' and that to do so is a desirable thing. This obscures the fundamental difference between prenatal testing and any other ways of preventing illness, namely that the 'treatment' which follows prenatal testing – abortion – 'cures' the condition by eliminating the foetus rather than by stopping the condition occurring in the first place.

The language of cure is also inappropriate because, as disability activist Simon Brisenden argued

> there is literally no case in which a disabled person should be seen as diseased, because no disease related to disability . . . extends so completely into a person's life as to define that person (Brisenden, 1987, p. 177).

Obstetrician Wendy Savage identifies another set of factors which indicate how the medical profession approaches prenatal screening and selective abortion. 'Medical people' she says

> feel quite strongly about prenatal screening programmes, since it's because of the advance in the medical knowledge that many handicapped people survive today. In the past, they wouldn't have survived, so nature had a way of ensuring that some handicapped people didn't survive, but we overcame that. So when people say 'how can you play God and decide which foetus is going to live or die' they forget that we have already changed the natural history by interfering after the baby is born. (Savage, 1988, p. 18)

What seems to be expressed here is the medical profession's ambivalent feelings as to whether their skills should always be used to enable disabled people to survive – and some sort of regret that they have been so used in the past. There is also an implied comparison between prenatal testing, avoiding the birth of a disabled baby, and the practice of withdrawing or withholding treatment to infants with Down's syndrome or spina bifida (Whitelaw, 1986). From the point of view of the profession, prenatal testing is 'the easier option'; whilst abortion is morally problematic, it is less so than bringing about the death of an infant. Furthermore, in name at least, the mother rather than the doctor is responsible for the decision as to whether or not to abort her disabled foetus, whereas it is the doctor who is ultimately responsible for the decision to withdraw/withhold treatment.

To the medical profession then, it appears that the case for prenatal testing is self-evident and largely unproblematic. It is a way of avoiding the difficulties of 'managing' those impairments not amenable to medical cure. However, other influential factors may also help to explain why prenatal screening programmes have been introduced and expanded at particular times. Firstly, professional interests have been served by the development of prenatal screening. For instance, in her historical study of medical care for pregnant women, Ann Oakley argues convincingly that antenatal care 'is nothing if women cannot be controlled'. In that context, prenatal testing can be seen as providing a reason for antenatal care to continue to be hospital based, thus ensuring a role for obstetricians, as well as by-passing the need for doctors, usually men, to rely on 'mere' women for information about the baby (Oakley, 1986). Farrant has shown that prenatal testing served as a lever to obtain government resources for screening facilities at a time of cutbacks in maternity care (Farrant, 1985).

That it is also the institutional context which creates doctors' support for the prevention of impairment rather than just medical attitudes, is confirmed by the fact that in some areas, the actions of doctors can cause impairment and yet these practices continue. I am thinking here of the 20 per cent incidence rate of impairment amongst babies treated in neonatal intensive care (Griffin, 1993).

Influencing women?

There is one further question to consider: what influence, if any, does the medical context of prenatal testing have on women's view of impairment and disability generally and their attitudes towards selective abortion in particular? There is little data available on this question and we should treat with caution the idea that the medical profession can impose their ideas on women. As Green and Statham's study of a small group of women who had undergone tests for Down's syndrome shows, most women want testing to be available (Green and Statham, 1993). More generally, it has been argued that any health programme which has as its aim the avoidance of illness, such as childhood immunisation programmes, will only be successful if they accord with cultural norms. There is no reason to think prenatal testing is any different in this respect. However, we can briefly explore the messages embedded in the practice of prenatal testing which may exert some influence on women.

While the aim of prenatal diagnosis is to offer women an informed choice, is there also an underlying expectation or pressure on women to abort an impaired foetus? Some obstetricians have been found to be reluctant to perform prenatal diagnosis on those women who would not consider abortion in the event of a positive result (d'A Crawfurd, 1983; Farrant, 1985).

This pressure to abort may also be integral to the structure and process of prenatal diagnosis itself. In other words,

> an offer of prenatal diagnosis implies a recommendation to accept that offer, which in turn entails a recommendation to terminate a pregnancy if it is found to show any abnormality. (Clarke, 1993, p. 1000)

The argument here is that because these offers are made by doctors in the context of an established medical procedure, they set off a 'likely chain of events in everyone's mind' (Clarke, 1993, p. 1001).

While this risks being too deterministic, the majority of research and development has focused on the technicalities of testing and the possibilities of preventing impairment rather than women's needs for support in making decisions. Thus the need for counselling and good information has been neglected (Green and Statham, 1993), and, as even the Royal College of Physicians has recognised, the psychological implications of selective abortion have been largely ignored (Royal College of Physicians, 1989).

It could be argued that prenatal testing has in a sense institutionalised the fear of impairment and increased the value attached to non-disabled children. The first question usually asked, and answered, immediately after birth is 'is the baby all right?' This question now dominates the early stages of pregnancy because most women now undergo some form of prenatal testing. Yet the number who will give birth to a disabled child is very small – less than 3 per cent (d'A Crawfurd, 1983). Prenatal testing may also raise unrealistic expectations of being able to avoid or control impairment: more than 90 per cent of childhood impairment occurs at or after birth and much is the result of environmental factors or accidents.

All this may be what have been called 'the unintended consequences of the application of technology' (Schwartz Cowan, 1992). It does seem that the institutional practice of prenatal testing systematically separates the normal from the 'abnormal', and brings into play a whole set of different judgements about the future for the latter as compared with the former. Some commentators have dubbed this 'quality control' (Rothman, 1989).

It is cruel to say so, but I believe that the value given to impaired foetuses is directly related to the extent to which women find the question of whether to abort on grounds of impairment a difficult one. One of the biggest dangers must surely be that the decision to abort becomes routine.

The scientific context of prenatal testing
Recent advances in the understanding of human genetics and reproductive technologies are providing new means of preventing impairment and disease. Anticipating these, in 1968, the American scientist Richard Sinshiemer coined the term

'New Eugenics'. This would guarantee 'to all human beings an individual and natural right, the right to health' (Fox Kellar, 1992, p. 294).

New eugenics emerged from the independent and 'pure' (as opposed to applied) genetic research which took place after the Second World War, unconnected to notions of racial purity. There is little evidence of the new eugenics, as a political ideology, being much more than the pronouncements of a few American scientists. However, the practical application of this new genetic knowledge through medical procedures such as prenatal testing, makes a form of human 'improvement' possible in a way that it has never been before. Thus the eugenic aim of 'improving the quality of the population' by eliminating supposedly bad characteristics, could happen without the need for state intervention or coercion.

There are, however, many questions to be considered about the notion of 'human improvement': does choosing to prevent the birth of someone with a genetic impairment really constitute 'human improvement'; who decides what constitutes a genetic characteristic which is harmful or beneficial to human improvement?

One concern here is that the institutional context of genetic research does not allow public discussion of these vital questions. There is a very close relationship between genetic research and medical practice: that is, new applications of genetic knowledge are put into medical practice – albeit on an experimental basis – as part of or quickly after the initial development stage, subject only to sanction by hospital ethics committees. The state has been reluctant to intrude because of the issues of clinical and research freedom involved. In the early 1980s, the government did come under pressure to consider the issue of embryology research and if and how it should be regulated. The result, six years after the Warnock Committee set up to deal with this question reported, was the 1990 Human Embryology and Fertilisation Act which I will consider in the next section. In this case, and in instances since then, such as the use of foetal eggs to treat infertile women, the issue only comes to public attention after the technologies have been developed.

The state has also been reluctant to intervene to limit the use of genetic technology as this has been seen as encroaching on the rights of individual choice. 'Human improvement' has been presented by scientists as 'a fact of life . . . because of consumer demand' (Kelves, 1992, p. 319). The issue here is not only whether people should have 'a right to chose' but perhaps how the terms of that choice are perceived and presented. By equating human improvement with consumer demand, there is a danger of reducing or undermining the moral seriousness of the choice.

The American sociologist, Troy Duster writes that

> Armed with individual choice, select Western nations will either have to confront the social control of this new [genetic] technology by explicit state devices, or watch social control be taken over inadvertently by the routine practice of social groups. (Duster, 1990, p. 35)

In other words, unless the state discusses or regulates the use of new genetic technology, debates 'what sort of people should be born' and the range of choices available, such issues will essentially be decided upon by the activities of the scientific and medical communities.

A further reason for concern is that the results of genetic research have the appearance of being objective facts about human existence. This overlooks the extent to which such research, and particularly the concept of genetic disease, is influenced by social prejudice and economic concerns. There is evidence that the choice of which disease or characteristic to try and link with a particular gene is a social decision influenced by social concerns. For example, some commentators have argued that attempts to find a genetic factor involved in coronary heart disease were influenced by the rising cost of health care for this condition (Duster, 1990). Individuals found to be at risk would be expected to take preventative measures. Such information also enables insurance companies to exclude high-risk groups from health care insurance.

Further, the very concept of genetic disease,

encompasses not only genetic disorders that are thought of as diseases but also genetic abnormalities associated with no known genetic disorders as well as disorders that may be neither genetic nor diseases (quoted in Fox Kellar, 1992, p. 291).

The very terms in which genetic research is presented are partial, and contribute to the idea that genetic impairment is both a definitive category and a wholly negative experience. A case in point is The Human Genome Project, which aims to identify the function of each gene and its relative position. The Project is seen as socially desirable and legitimate because of the search to find genes responsible for particular medical conditions. Popular discussion of the Project has led to talk of 'good' or normal genes, which define what it is to be human, and 'bad' genes which cause diseases, and, by implication, those that are 'abnormal' or less than human. This is at best an oversimplification, which while it may make complex scientific ideas accessible, obscures the fact that each human being has a unique genome, and genetic variation is vital to our continued survival. Moreover, as *Science* journalist Tom Wilkie points out,

> there is a legitimate worry that such an emphasis on humanity's genetic constitution may distort our sense of values, and lead us to forget that human life is more than just the expression of a genetic programme written in the chemistry of DNA. (Wilkie, 1993, p. 3)

The risks associated with the way genetic research is developing are insidious, coming less from explicit eugenic intent or threat of compulsion than from overlooking the collective consequences of individual actions, and letting the political and medical agenda be set by what science has now enabled us to do. As we shall see, this is already happening.

Prenatal testing and public policy
In this section, I want to focus on the broader policy and political issues involved in prenatal testing.

The politics of impairment prevention

Since the late 1970s, health policy makers have focused much attention on developing strategies aimed at health maintenance, enabling people to stay healthy. They were motivated to do so by, on the one hand, rising government expenditure on health at a time of economic crisis and on the other, the health status of the population remaining relatively static despite such expenditure.

In this policy context, prenatal diagnosis could be viewed as a medical procedure which was developed at an apposite time to receive both state funding and medical support. Improvements in antibiotics and social conditions mean infectious diseases now rarely lead to childhood impairment or death. So genetic and congenital conditions accounted for a much greater proportion of childhood impairment. Prenatal diagnosis offered a means of reducing the incidence of such impairments. Moreover, several features of prenatal testing made it easier to implement than other health promotion policies, such as encouraging people to stop smoking. Prenatal testing had a measurable and definite outcome, indicating an efficient use of state resources, it provided a clear role for the medical profession and could use existing health structures. None of these were true for health education. In addition, prenatal testing provided a visible sign of the state's commitment to women's health care, at a time when such a commitment was being questioned.

The general aim of preventing impairment by prenatal testing and subsequent abortion was politically convenient in the context of broader health priorities, and continued to be insofar as this aim was written into maternity policy throughout the 1980s. However, this contrasts with the government's reluctance to adopt measures which would prevent foetal impairment in the first place. For example, if women took folic acid just before or just after conception, the occurrence of neural tube defects could be reduced by 75 per cent. The current government unsuccessfully urged the Federation of British Bakers to add folic acid to bread as the surest way of ensuring that all women got sufficient quantities. Legislation requiring bakers to do so would be contrary to the government's stance on the deregulation of industry. The commitment to prevention, therefore, is seldom absolute but dependent on the interests at stake in the particular means of prevention under consideration.

The 1990 Human Fertilisation and Embryology Act – a new approach?

The policy structure governing prenatal diagnosis had originally been split between health policy, and legislation regulating abortion. In neither was the use of prenatal diagnosis a substantive issue. These two strands were brought together in the 1990 Human Fertilisation and Embryology Act. Ostensibly, this was a matter of parliamentary convenience rather than principle – two separate reports, The Warnock Report (1985) and the deliberations of the Brightman Committee (1988) on the upper time limit for abortion required legislative time. However, the issue which linked them both was the moral and ethical limits to the use of new reproductive technologies to prevent impairment.

Some commentators have argued that the 1990 Act represented a response to medical interests. MPs voted to allow research on embryos up to 14 days old because

medical advances . . . made the detection and tentative treatment of genetic disease and chromosomal disorders much more readily available. They [MPs] were mindful that when it came to the implementation of these technological advances, i.e. abortion of affected foetuses, they were talking about the elimination of the problem through the elimination of the patient. This they felt much securer in accepting if strong medical grounds could be adduced in support. (Morgan and Lee, 1991, p. 40)

One can understand why MPs felt on securer ground with medical support, given the weight accorded to medical opinion in such matters. It is, however, somewhat ironic, given the apparent reluctance of the profession to discuss the ethical issues involved with prenatal diagnosis that we noted earlier. Further, it is surely a political rather than a medical question whether society wants to sanction or prohibit the 'elimination of the problem'.

The 1990 Act also changed the upper time limits for abortion. The 1967 Abortion Act had not specified an upper time limit in terms of gestational age. Rather the provision of the earlier, 1929 Infant Life Preservation Act, that it would be an offence to procure or cause an abortion, if a child was capable of being born alive, applied to abortions carried out under the 1967 Act. As neonatal medicine improved, so the gestational age at which a child was capable of being born alive, reduced. To err on the side of caution the upper limit to abortion was usually taken to be two weeks less than that at which it was currently thought possible for a child to be capable of being born alive.

By the late 1980s, medical technology made it possible for foetuses born at 24 weeks to survive and there was pressure to introduce a specified time limit for abortions which would reflect these advances. However if the limit was reduced, as proposed in 1988, to 24 weeks, this might give insufficient time for selective abortion, as prenatal diagnostic results were often not available before 22 to 23 weeks. The issue had become how to accommodate what had become technically possible – prenatal testing – within our existing moral and political framework – that abortion should only be permissible, in certain circumstances, before the point at which the foetus becomes viable. Such a pragmatic approach prevented the broader and political implications from being explored.

A House of Lords Select Committee, under the Chairmanship of Lord Brightman, was appointed in 1988 to consider the issue of abortion time limits. It recommended the removal of the time limit altogether where an abortion was carried out under Section 4 of the 1967 Act, the foetal impairment grounds. Thus

> If, for example, an unborn child were diagnosed as grossly abnormal and unable to lead any meaningful life . . . in the opinion of the Committee . . . there is no logic in requiring the mother to carry to full term because the diagnosis was made too late. (House of Lords, 1988, p. 18)

There was little attempt during the course of the Committee's deliberations to ascertain which impairments, if any, prohibited a 'meaningful life' or the broader consequences of allowing abortion to term. They seemed rather to accept their own apparent horror of impairment and consequently wished to facilitate its prevention wherever possible.

Interestingly, a joint report submitted to the Committee by the Royal College of Physicians and Royal College of Obstetricians and Gynaecologists recommended a 24-week limit under Section 1 – the so-called 'social grounds' – and a 28-week limit under Section 4 – grounds of foetal handicap. While the Brightman Committee rejected the Royal Colleges' recommendation (on the grounds given in the quote above), the government in fact incorporated it into the Bill presented to Parliament.

However, an amendment to remove the 28-week upper limit on Section 4 was introduced and supported by David Alton and Anne Widdecombe, two prominent anti-abortion MPs. They did so, in effect, as part of a 'parliamentary deal' to secure the third reading of the Bill. In return for this, 'pro-choice' MPs agreed to vote to lower the time limit to 24 weeks for Section 1, and also for Sections 2 and 3 which concerned situations where the mother's life or health were at risk (House of Commons Official Report, 22 April 1990).

In a later debate Widdecombe sought to reintroduce the time limit, apparently having not realised that the provisions of the Infant Life Preservation Act – i.e. the 'capable of being alive' test – would no longer apply. Her amendment failed but the debate revealed that one of the main concerns was the definition of 'serious handicap'. (House of Commons Official Report, 21 June 1990). It was agreed that this should be monitored by requiring medical practitioners to state the nature of the handicap that the foetus was at risk from on the official abortion certificate.

So, the fact that the clause permitting abortion to term on grounds of serious handicap was passed was due to a mixture of political expediency and the persuasiveness of prevention of impairment. Two legal commentators on reproductive issues, Morgan and Lee conclude the UK has now a much more explicitly based eugenic abortion policy than before 1990, not just in the sense that abortion on the ground of foetal abnormality is to be readily available, after 28 weeks, but also because it was apparent that the most clearly favoured ground for abortion was the genetic handicap ground. (Morgan and Lee, 1989, p. 41)

The concern here is one of principle – that impairment has become reason for affording a foetus less protection, and less value before the law. There is also a political concern; why can rights be removed so easily in the name of prevention? How can disabled people be confident that they will be protected from the implications or risks of new reproductive technologies?

Very recently, there seems to have been another shift in policy, which has worrying eugenic resonances. In a recent report to the Cabinet from a Task Force on Genetic Screening, the emphasis on prevention for its own sake was very much in evidence. It wrote

Serum screening for Down's syndrome, for example, can detect over 60 per cent of affected pregnancies and its effective implementation would have more impact than any other in reducing the prevalence of severe mental retardation. (Advisory Council on Science and Technology, 1993, p. 43)

There was no intimation that 'effective implementation' depended on women 'opting' to have a termination in the event of a positive diagnosis. The Report went on to recommend the establishment of a Central Screening Office, to provide better coordination and implementation of all genetic screening programmes and prenatal diagnosis. This echoes an argument that prenatal diagnosis should be seen as a public health function, receiving funding nationally rather than having to compete with other services for funding at a local level.

A national programme may make sense in terms of equitable provision and the effective dissemination of knowledge.

But it risks giving undue emphasis to the aim of prevention and compromising the aim of offering women an informed choice. There is also something disconcerting, almost eugenic, about avoidance of impairment being seen as a public health measure. It is not, of course, infectious and indeed not an illness, in the sense that it becomes part of, rather than disrupts, normal life. 'Public Health' implies that impairment damages and disrupts the community as a whole, and that its prevention is as much in the interests of the community as the individual.

Choice or Economics?

Finally, I want to consider briefly, if and how the state's interests in prenatal diagnosis, particularly its economic interests, impinge upon the explicit aim of prenatal diagnosis, namely, to enable women to make informed choices (Royal College of Physicians, 1989).

To demonstrate the effectiveness of prenatal diagnosis, cost benefit analyses were undertaken by health economists, to confirm that resources invested in screening would be offset by savings or 'benefits'. A major item of 'benefit' in these was a calculation of the savings to the state of the cost of supporting a disabled child. (Methodologically, such calculations were very difficult and there was no consensus amongst economists about how they should be done.) Such analyses implied or perhaps illustrated that the state's interest in prenatal testing is not in women making any choice, but in making a choice to have an abortion: the benefits and justification for expenditure on prenatal diagnosis would only accrue if she chose to abort following a positive result.

One has to be wary of interpreting this economic interest too literally, of the state pressurising women to chose abortions following a positive test result. Any money saved by testing programmes is notional, and does not appear as extra money in health budgets. However, I think this interest has an ideological function, which impinges both on women and disabled people.

Press reporting of prenatal diagnosis tends to quote the 'lifetime' costs of a disabled person, as do MPs in parliamentary debates on abortion. For example

> The private financial burden of caring for a severely
> handicapped child has been estimated by the courts as
> £500,000. If one takes into account the cost to the state of
> the statutory provision, the cost would well be another
> £500,000 . . . Why should the House consider forcing people
> to accept such a burden if they do not want it? (Hansard, 22
> January 1988)

The emphasis on the economic advantages for both women
and the state almost always presents an open and shut case
that prenatal diagnosis is the best way the 'burden' of
impairment could be shared. It implies that the state support
extends to offering prenatal diagnosis but not to sharing the
'burden' through innovative and flexible support services
which would give real choice. Therefore, the fear becomes
that if a woman decides not to have a test, or to continue with
pregnancy despite a positive result, it is her responsibility for
which she must pay.

This continued reference to the cost to the state and to
women is, first of all, something of an insult to disabled people.
It fails to recognize the many different roles which disabled
people do play in society, despite obstacles which prevent
them doing so, or to acknowledge that many other categories
of people cost the state a good deal of money in the course of
their lifetime. It also implies that disabled people's claim on the
state should be cash limited – and moreover, that this limit has
been passed. This is insidious, especially when the 'solution'
on offer is abortion. Indirectly, it may also be one means
of deflecting demands for much needed community care
services. At a time when the government emphasises public
expenditure restraint, seeing disabled people as 'expensive
burdens' contributes to a climate where the legitimacy of
providing support services is questioned.

There would seem to be a precariously thin line dividing the
aim of preventing impairment in the interests of society,
which could be eugenic in effect if not intent, from the aims of
enabling women to make an informed choice and preventing
individual suffering caused by impairment. The feminist
scientist, Ruth Hubbard has argued that

Women are expected to implement society's eugenic prejudices by 'choosing' to have the appropriate test, and . . .
'electing' to terminate if it looks as though the outcome will
offend. (Hubbard, 1986, p. 240)

Thus it would seem that the threat of eugenics comes not
from any explicit compulsion or coercion, but from the
expectations and economic constraints which set tight parameters on women's choice. Such parameters are set, it seems,
without any real debate at either the policy or clinical level.

Conclusion
What emerges from all this is complexity and confusion. On
the one hand, the complexity means it is difficult to interpret
the use and development of prenatal testing as having an
explicitly eugenic intent or even as a considered policy
response to disability. On the other the confusion means that
the social and collective consequences of prenatal testing too
easily go unnoticed and undiscussed. Indeed the charge of 'lack
of discussion' would seem to be a recurring theme.

From this very confusion and these complexities, it is
difficult to pinpoint the particular implications for disabled
people. Undoubtedly, the way policy is discussed around
prenatal testing often shows – at best – considerable ignorance
about disability and impairment. Morever, the implications of
the possibilities of the new genetic knowledge are as yet
unknown. Arguably, there is reason to be fearful. Not,
so much, of the curtailing of rights or freedoms, but of
unleashing a power to alter life – and death – without having
identified the mechanisms or means to discuss whether this is
desirable or where to place the limits on its use. Further, there
is considerable scope for oppressive ideas of normality and
what it is to be human, which are given a particular force by
genetic research, to inform the political, scientific and medical
decision-making processes.

So, as a disabled woman concerned with both disabled
people's and women's interests, what recommendations
would I make about future policy on prenatal testing and
genetic knowledge?

First, I would reiterate that any decision to undergo testing or to opt for abortion should rest wth the woman. More attention needs to be paid to the ways that those choices are constrained both by social circumstances and the experience of testing itself. The greater the scope for choice (within the confines of the abortion law), and the more support the woman has, the less danger of abortion on grounds of impairment becoming routine and expected. In particular, there is a need for much research, imagination and sensitivity concerning the provision of information about impairments following a positive diagnosis. Such information has to tread a fine line between giving an overly optimistic or overly pessimistic view. Both lead to disappointment and decisions which are guided by incomplete and/or inaccurate information.

Second, there should be greater discussion at all stages of the research and implementation of prenatal testing. Politicians, scientists and doctors alike must recognise that disabled people do have a particular interest in prenatal testing and should therefore be systematically involved in debates about prenatal testing. This would provide some general insights into the complexities of the experience of disability and impairment, and help to correct many of the current misconceptions. This is not to say that disabled people's voice should be decisive, but it must be represented. It should be noted that many of the traditional disability pressure groups have a conflict of loyalties here because they often have a large membership of parents. The views of disabled people and parents may well conflict, and it is vital that both are separately represented.

Third, there should be far greater vigilance to ensure that what is made possible by new genetic research does not lead to the abandoning of fundamental political and moral principles. For this reason, I would recommend that the upper time limit for abortion on grounds of 'serious handicap' should be lowered to 24 weeks, notwithstanding the fact that 'serious handicap' is, in practice, being narrowly defined. The fact that there is a piece of legislation on the statute books which abandons the fundamental principle of equity of law is a dangerous precedent. Arguably, it confirms or adds to the general low esteem in which disabled people are held. More concretely, the benefits of preventing the suffering of women giving birth to a child with a fatal impairment must be weighed against recent reports that foetuses aborted at 27 weeks are surviving for several hours after birth (Weale, 1994). This must cause much private grief. It also blurs the dividing line of birth and thus creates further moral uncertainties.

My fourth recommendation would underpin the above three, by confirming that disabled people, whatever their impairment, are an integral part of society and should be afforded the same respect and dignity as other human beings. That recommendation is that the current demand of disabled people for comprehensive civil rights legislation should be met. This would not, of course, rule out the use of prenatal testing or the dangers of the new genetic knowledge. However, it would provide a much clearer framework against which those tests and dangers could be judged.

References

Advisory Council on Science and Technology (1993) *Report on medical research and health: Task force on screening, diagnosis and prevention*, Cabinet Office.

Anderson, E. *et al.* (1982) *Disability in Adolescence*, Methuen.

Bennet, P. (1993) 'Ethics and late termination of pregnancy', Letter to Editor, *Lancet*, 9 October, p. 929.

Brisenden, Simon (1986) 'Independence and Disability', in *Disability Handicap and Society*, Vol. 1, No. 2.

Burleigh, Michael (1994) *Death and Deliverance: 'Euthanasia' in Germany*, Cambridge.

Clarke, A. (1993) 'Is non-directive genetic counselling possible?', in *Lancet*, 19 October, pp. 998–1002.

Davis, A. (1985), 'Abortion and disability – whose oppression?' in *Peace News*, 14 June, pp. 12–14.

Davis, A. (1987), 'Women with disabilities: abortion and liberation', in *Disability Handicap & Society*, Vol 2, No. 3.

Duster, T. (1990) *Backdoor to Eugenics*, Routledge.

d'A Crawfurd, M. (1983) 'Ethical and legal aspects of early diagnosis', in *British Medical Bulletin*, Vol. 39, No. 4, pp. 302–7.

Farrant, W. (1985) 'Who's for amniocentesis? The politics of prenatal screening', in H. Homans, ed., *The Sexual Politics of Reproduction*, Gower.

Finger, A. (1984) 'Claiming all our bodies: reproductive rights and disability', in Arditti, R., Duelli Klien, R. and Minden, S., *Test Tube Women: What Future for Motherhood?*', Pandora.

Fox Kellar, E. (1992) 'Nature, nurture and the Human Genome Project', in Kelves, D. J. and Hood, L. eds, *The Code of Codes*, Harvard University Press.

Gallagher, Hugh (1990) *By Trust Betrayed: Patients, physicians and the license to kill in the Third Reich*, Henry Holt.

Glasman, C. (1991) 'Disability, embryology, abortion in Great Britain', in *Women's Health and Reproductive Rights Information Centre: Newsletter*, July.

Glasman, C. (1987) 'Abortion is killing, but without it there looms the 24 hour a day job of motherhood', in *Disability Now*, November.

Green, J. and Statham, H. (1993) 'Serum screening for Down's syndrome: some women's experiences', *British Medical Journal*, Vol. 307, pp. 174–6.

Griffin, J. (1993) *Born Too Soon*, Office of Health Economics.

Hannaford, S. (1985) *Living Outside Inside*, Canterbury Press, Berkeley, California.

House of Lords (1988) *Report of Select Committee on Infant Life Preservation Bill*, 15 February, Hansard.

House of Commons Official Report (1990) *Human Fertilisation and Embryology Bill*, 22 April, Hansard.

House of Commons Official Report (1990) *Human Fertilisation and Embryology Bill*, 21 June, Hansard.

House of Commons Official Report (1988) *Abortion (Amendment Bill)*, *2nd Reading*, 22 January, Hansard.

Hubbard, R. (1986), 'Eugenics and prenatal testing', in *International Journal of Health Services*, Vol. 16, No. 2. pp. 227–42.

Kelves, D. J. (1985) *In the Name of Eugenics*, Penguin.

Kelves, D. J. (1992) 'Reflections' in Kelves, D. J. and Hood, L., eds., *The Code of Codes*, Harvard University Press.

Lilford, P. and Thornton, E. (1993) 'Ethics and late termination of pregnancy', Letters to Editor, *Lancet*, 29 August, p. 499.

Morgan, D. and Lee, R. (1989) *Birthrights*, Routledge.

Morgan, D. and Lee, R. (1991) *A Guide to the Human Fertilisation and Embryology Act 1990*, Blackwell.

Morris, Jenny (1991) *Pride Against Prejudice: Transforming Attitudes to Disability*, The Women's Press.

Oakley, A. (1986) *The Captured Womb: a history of the medicalization of pregnant women*, Blackwell.

Proctor, Robert (1988) *Racial Hygiene: Medicine under the Nazis*, Harvard University Press.

Rothman, Barbara Katz (1984) 'The meaning of choice in reproductive technology', in Arditti, R., Duelli Klien, R. and Minden, S., *Test Tube Women: What Future for Motherhood?*, Pandora.

Rothman, Barbara Katz (1989) *The Tentative Pregnancy: prenatal diagnosis and the future of motherhood*, Unwin and Hyman.

Royal College of Physicians (1989) *Prenatal Diagnosis and Genetic Screening: community and service implications*, Royal College of Physicians.

Savage, Wendy (1988) 'Whose right to life: a round table discussion', in *Marxism Today*, July.

Saxton, M (1984) 'Born and unborn, the implications of reproductive technology', in Arditti, R., Duelli Klien, R. and Minden, S., *Test Tube Women: What Future for Motherhood?*, Pandora.

Schwartz Cowan, Ruth (1992) 'Genetic technology and reproductive choice', in Kelves D. J. & Hood, L., eds., *The Code of Codes*, Harvard University Press.

Seller, M. (1990) 'Is antenatal selection for spina bifida possible?' in *British Medical Journal*, 4 August, pp. 231–51.

Weale, S. (1994) 'Foetus was aborted after scan error', *Guardian* 3 June.

Whitelaw, A. (1986) 'Death as an option in neonatal intensive care', *Lancet*, 9 August, pp. 328–31.

Wilkie, E. (1987) 'Pre-birth disposal is not the answer', in *Disability Now*, November.

Wilkie, E. (1989) 'Reflections', in Alton, D., *Whose choice is it anyway?*, Marshall, Morgan and Scott.

Wilkie, T. (1993) *Perilous Knowledge*, Faber and Faber.

Wolfson Institute (n.d.) *Maternal Serum Screening Test for Down's syndrome and Open Neural Tube Defects*, Leaflet, Wolfson Institute.

CHAPTER EIGHT

DOCTOR, DOCTOR ...
Disabled Women's Experience of
General Practitioners
Nasa Begum

Women with arthritis seem to inspire either irritation or boredom in some GPs ... if one doesn't have the strength to do verbal combat one quietly leaves having wasted one's time and energy, and depressed oneself by getting nowhere.

Introduction
Whenever a group of disabled women meet together, sooner or later we end up discussing the medical profession and our experiences of health services. This chapter was borne out of one such discussion, when one woman commented that disabled women had so many concerns about health services that we could write a book. Whilst tackling the whole of the medical world seemed a relevant but unenviable task, I decided to limit myself to exploring disabled women's experiences of general practitioners.

Whether it is for biological or socially constructed reasons women in general visit their doctors more, they are more likely to be taking medication than men, and they carry greater responsibility for other people's health (Roberts, 1985). Studies of women's health have revealed concerns about the quality and quantity of health services available to women and the social control aspects of medicine. They have documented how the medical profession controls the lives of women and defines what is acceptable and unacceptable conduct. Helen Roberts explains:

> Women and doctors (even if those doctors are women) don't just have subtly different viewpoints about health, they inhabit different worlds. Doctors have the power to define what is, and what is not, illness, what is and what is not appropriate behaviour in a patient; and what is to go on in the consulting room. (Roberts, 1985, p. 2)

Work on women's experiences as providers and receivers of health services highlights problems and difficulties with a medical world predominantly occupied by men and defined by male perceptions of 'normality'. However, whilst there has been some acknowledgement that definitions of 'normality' and experience of the medical world may be determined by how the additional dimensions of race, class, and age interact to shape women's lives, there has been no analysis of the role of disability in women's experience of health and health care services.

In the past, disabled people have fought so hard to challenge the medicalisation of their lives and experiences that concerns about health needs have tended to be minimised. The often oppressive nature of medical treatment, and a resistance to disability being construed as a catalogue of medical problems has made disabled people wary of putting health issues on the public and/or academic agenda. Whilst this may be an understandable response to the intrusive and often interventionist nature of the medical world, the fact remains that disabled people, whether as a result of impairment or as a consequence of everyday illnesses, are consumers of health services. As Margaret Lloyd points out

> . . . the narrow defining of disability as clinical conditions results in an all-pervasiveness of doctors' power over disabled people's lives, of which the power to make decisions about fitness for work and entitlement to welfare benefits are but examples. This does not *necessarily* mean, however,

that the medical aspects of their lives are unimportant for disabled people. (Lloyd, 1992, p. 211).

The authority and control which the medical profession exercises over the lives of disabled people inevitably has a profound impact on both disabled men and disabled women. Nevertheless disabled people are not a homogenous group and factors such as race, class, age, sexuality, sex and gender often play a significant role in shaping their experiences of health services. Black people, for example, have drawn attention to the way misguided perceptions of people with sickle-cell anaemia as 'drug addicts' often prevent access to the health services. Disabled women have raised concerns about the way rehabilitation programmes place an emphasis on 'cultivating competitive attitudes' and have addressed concerns about male sexuality and male employment (Morris 1989, 1994; Matthews, 1983). Much more work remains to be done on how disability interacts with other dimensions of social inequality to influence people's experiences of health care.

There is now an established body of literature exploring the way sexist ideology in the medical world often underpins women's experience of health services, yet disabled women do not feature in any of these discussions. This chapter is an attempt to place disabled women's experience of health and health care on the feminist agenda by exploring one aspect of this experience – their contact with general practitioners.

How I went about doing this research

Initially, I aimed to carry out in-depth interviews with a small number of women in order to establish the nature of disabled women's relationships with their general practitioners. Advertisements were placed in the disability press, inviting women to contact me if they were willing to take part in the study by completing a questionnaire or participating in a face to face interview. It was envisaged that a very short questionnaire with a series of open-ended questions could be designed to obtain an idea of the types of issues that concerned disabled women. This would be followed up with a small number of qualitative interviews.

The response to the advertisements was overwhelming. Over 100 women throughout the country responded to the advertisement and 3 organisations asked for multiple copies of the questionnaire. The telephone discussions and letters received about the research clearly showed that disabled women's experience of GPs was a major area of concern for them.

In order to utilise the experience of all the women who expressed an interest in the research, a decision was made to develop the questionnaire further, so that it could be circulated to everyone, and also to use it as a postal questionnaire. Women who could not fill in the questionnaire were offered the opportunity to take part in a telephone discussion, have a face to face interview or receive practical support to fill it in.

The questionnaire was designed to incorporate quantitative and qualitative information. Its primary aim was to explore the experiences of disabled women rather than investigate the characteristics of the GP or the GP's practice. It included open-ended questions about current and previous GPs. A total of 80 completed questionnaires were returned by the deadline set.

Limitations of the research
Most empirical research has its limitations; either because of the methodology used, or by the very nature of the subject matter itself, and sometimes a range of other unexpected factors. This research was no exception. Although it was not meant to be a representative study, the mere fact that it relied on self-selection built an inherent bias into the sample, as it inevitably attracted disabled women who wanted to share their experience of GPs. Also, relying on questionnaires as the main tool of the research excluded some disabled women, particularly women for whom written English is not their preferred method of communication. If this work is developed further it would be important to use what Mike Oliver calls an emancipatory research paradigm (Oliver, 1992) with a particular emphasis on group discussions and semi-structured interviews to target disabled women who have not been properly represented at this stage.

The emphasis of the research was on setting an agenda from disabled women's perspective, and there is therefore very little information about the women's GPs, the type of practice they work in, frequency of contact and so on. In retrospect it may have been useful to explore information about the characteristics of GPs further. Nevertheless the material elicited from the research provides a useful starting point for highlighting a neglected area of experience.

Finally the study does not incorporate any comparative work with non-disabled women or disabled men. It is clear that many of the issues raised are not unique to disabled women. However the central thrust of this research is to demonstrate the extent to which GPs can shape the lives of disabled women, and to highlight the urgent need to include them in the discussions about women's health, primary health care and disabled people's use of health services.

Characteristics of the women who responded

The women who responded were fairly well distributed geographically with 43 per cent living in a city, 33 per cent in a town and 20 per cent in a village. Almost a third of the sample lived alone. Thirty per cent lived with a partner, 14 per cent with a partner and children, 7 per cent lived with their children, and another 7 per cent lived with other family members. Only one person stated that they lived in a residential home so this is one group who are clearly under-represented in this study.

Only 4 per cent of the sample did not identify their sexuality. The other 96 per cent comprised of 5 per cent lesbians, 9 per cent bi-sexual women and 82 per cent heterosexual women. Given that it is estimated that 1 in 10 of the population are not heterosexual, the research appears to encompass a fairly representative proportion of lesbian and bi-sexual women.

Just over half (52 per cent) of the women had children. This figure includes those whose children were grown up and had left home, as well as those whose children were still living with them.

African-Caribbean women formed 5 per cent of the sample,

Asian women 2 per cent, and UK European women 84 per cent. It is difficult to know the proportion of Black disabled women in the population. Although their representation in this study may seem reasonable in theoretical terms, it has not ensured Black disabled women are a significant proportion of the sample.

Approximately two-thirds of the women were between the ages of 21 and 49 years, while only 14 per cent were between the ages of 50 and 59 and another 14 per cent over 60. The government's survey of disabled people indicated that the largest proportion of disabled women are over the age of 60 (OPCS, 1988). In contrast, this sample appears to mainly represent women whose impairments to a large extent are not part of the ageing process.

Twenty-nine per cent of the women were born with an impairment, another 17 per cent became disabled before the age of 22, while the remainder acquired their impairment later in adult life.

The majority of women described their impairment as a physical condition with multiple sclerosis accounting for 20 per cent, back/spinal injuries experienced by 12 per cent and arthritis/osteoarthritis by 11 per cent. Deaf women only formed 3 per cent of the sample and blind women totalled 5 per cent, although 22 per cent indicated that their impairment affected their sight.

Registering with a General Practitioner

Ninety-four per cent of the women were registered with a GP. Almost half (49 per cent) of the sample had been registered with their current GP between 1 and 10 years, with another 46 per cent being registered for more than 10 years. Only 3 per cent of the women had been with their doctors less than a year.

The most common reason (55 per cent) for registering with a GP was the proximity of the surgery. Just over a third (38 per cent) of the women identified reputation as the reason they registered with their current doctor, while gender and accessibility were only cited as a reason for selecting a GP by 28 per cent and 30 per cent of the sample respectively. In contrast when women were asked about the factors that were important when looking for a new GP, accessibility (62 per cent), reputation (64 per cent), location (59 per cent) and gender (41 per cent) featured strongly. This probably reflects a mismatch between what disabled women are seeking and the reality of what is available. The factors identified as important in finding a GP may have little bearing on who they eventually register with because options can be limited from the outset.

The actual process of finding a doctor can be quite an arduous task. Although Family Health Services Authorities may hold details about GPs, often information about physical access and other important facilities for disabled women can be limited. Finding a suitable doctor can be a matter of pot luck. Nora recounted how when she moved house

> the Family Practitioner Committee were very unhelpful when I asked them for details of the nearest doctor with an accessible surgery. They sent me a list of local GPs, and suggested that I went round looking at surgeries until I found one that was accessible. I went out armed with a map and did just that. I was fortunate that this haphazard method found me the best GP I have ever had.

General practices usually have 'catchment areas' in that they will only take people on who live within a particular distance from the surgery. This can restrict people's ability to choose a GP. Although proximity of the surgery to where they live was important for the women in this study, it was clear that some will travel greater distances to find a supportive GP. Roseanne was lucky enough to be able to change to a practice further away from her home. She explained,

> I travel five miles to my GP's practice instead of a quarter mile to the village practice who were my previous GPs. The reason for this is because I really trust my current practice. All of the GPs are helpful and there is good communication between them. They have a human approach which makes a difference knowing that you are considered as a person rather than just another patient.

Some women said that they would not change their doctor because of the difficulties of finding someone else: 'I would not ever consider changing my GP because I don't think I'd find another GP to take me on', wrote Joni. 'At least my present GP knows my history and although he doesn't do anything unless I ask, he doesn't ignore me completely. I think he is sympathetic and believes in me when he sees me.' When women do have to change their GP they often view this with great trepidation. As Jennifer wrote, 'It has taken me a long time to find a GP who listened and believed me. I now have to try and find another one and I am not looking forward to this.'

Contact with General Practitioners

The most common purpose cited for contacting a doctor was to obtain repeat prescriptions, or for issues relating to impairment.

Contact with General Practitioners

Percentage of women contacting GP for following reasons:

Reason for contact	%
Repeat prescriptions	84
Issues relating to impairment	60
Referral to other health services	56
Authorisation for other services	51
Colds/flu/general poor health	48
Medical reports	41
Pain control	41
Breast/cervical screening	37
Children's health	19
Menopause	16
Contraception	10
Maternity services	5
Other	15

Note: Women gave more than one reason for contacting GPs.

Referral to other health services, authorisation for non-medical resources and services, and the writing of medical reports were also common reasons for contacting a GP in this sample. It was clear from the women's comments that a GP's support in these matters was often very important. Roseanne talks about how supportive her GP had been in terms of making helpful referrals to other health services: 'When I first became debilitated with chronic pain and had come to realise that I wasn't going to "get better", my GP was great and did not give me the "pull yourself together" nonsense that I got from the hospital consultant. He tried various drugs, spent time with me and referred me without qualm to the homeopathic hospital.'

Nora wrote:

I use a wheelchair full-time. The local hospital trust refused to give me a new wheelchair as I hadn't had my present one for five years – I was told if it was worn out I had abused it! I repeated this conversation to my GP. He said 'leave it it me'. I had a new wheelchair 10 days later. (No explanation from trust why they had changed their mind).

Izzy reported a similarly helpful attitude on the part of her doctor: 'He agrees that I can lead a better life with help from services and therefore will go to great lengths to ensure that I get what I require.'

On the other hand, a number of women reported difficulties in the referral process. Rachel wrote about how her GP's 'remarks in these [hospital referral] letters make my problems sound very trivial, i.e. "has headaches and refused medication". In fact, I had tried about 12 different medications over as many years with side effects and the pain is intolerable. It now seems that my spine has crushed into my skull and I have had to be referred to a senior neurologist ... After 14 years of this getting worse monthly.'

Women also wrote about how their access to specialists is dependent on the knowledge and beliefs of individual GPs. For example, Elizabeth wrote about how her GP has been 'helpful in that he referred me to an allergy specialist early on in my illness who is one of the few consultants to accept ME as a serious illness. Unhelpful in that he will not refer me to any alternative practitioner, e.g. homeopathic doctor which he dismisses as cranky.'

GPs are used extensively as the passport to other non-medical resources or activities. Figure 1 shows a breakdown of the type of things GPs had to provide reports for:

Figure 1: GP Reports as a Passport to Daily Living Requirements

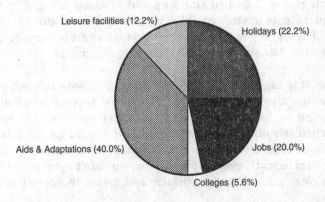

Leisure facilities (12.2%)
Holidays (22.2%)
Aids & Adaptations (40.0%)
Jobs (20.0%)
Colleges (5.6%)

Doctors have a tendency to focus on functional impairment and to make assumptions about ability and competence with little reference to the environmental, economic and attitudinal barriers that may be more important. These attitudes have wide-ranging significance for disabled people when they require medical reports in order to assess employment and leisure facilities. A number of respondents expressed concern about the extent to which doctors could shape their lives and opportunities. Emma wrote

Previously I had a female GP, but she had a very naff attitude towards disability. Every visit for cold or flu I used to be told to stop working, I shouldn't bother to work due to my disability. Always assumed that I wouldn't be working, even though I had told her I work a number of times.

Many disabled women have to go through a process of medical screening before they take up employment, and it is rather worrying that a GP's perception of a disabled woman's 'employability' can be a deciding factor. Moreover, there may be specific values and beliefs held about certain groups of disabled women such as lesbians, black women or women with learning difficulties which can exacerbate the difficulties experienced by disabled women generally. Daniella points out

> GPs have the power to allow people with learning difficulties to fully participate in society . . . My GP has abused his power. I had to stand up and advocate my ability to participate in student holidays, jobs and travel abroad. My GP was going to take my rights away from me because of his assumptions of people with learning difficulties.

A doctor can have a crucial influence on a woman's opportunities. Eve's GP had to write medical reports when she applied to be approved as an adoptive mother. 'He was particularly disturbed by the idea of me adopting a child, and seemed to go out of his way to mention my blindness on the medical reports, even in places where it didn't seem to apply. He clearly saw it as an obstacle and meant to portray it as such.'

Difficulties in the relationship between disabled women and their GPs

Forty per cent of the women said that they experience difficulties when they have face to face contact with their current GP. High though this percentage is, it is still an understatement as a number of women who did not tick the box on the questionnaire indicating that they faced difficulties with their GP wrote about problems when responding to open-ended questions. Access problems and negative attitudes were cited as the most common sources of difficulty.

Access Barriers

To a large extent access barriers are associated with people in wheelchairs and some Family Health Services Authorities have taken measures to address the physical barriers of steps, the width of doors and so on. However physical access goes far beyond the bricks and mortar of buildings. Penny usually has home visits from her GP, partly because she has no transport to get to the doctor and partly because of the lack of facilities at the surgery. She wrote, '. . . I have no transport – sight problems prevent me driving now and we have no wheelchair accessible transport here. The surgery also has no accessible toilet or adjustable couch, though it is designed with ramp entrance and horrendously heavy doors.' And Chris talked of her 'group practice with new, supposedly accessible, surgery which has a nasty slope in the car park and a steep ramp'. Roseanne mentioned that 'access is quite difficult if I have my baby with me as it is through awkward double doors. There is no provision for orange badge holders in the car park.'

Women with visual impairments often find there is very little recognition of their access needs. Lisa explains 'The GP I am registered with . . . is always aloof and keeps very silent, which is the worst thing for a visually impaired person to deal with . . .' Sharon points out 'When I visit the surgery no one ever shows me to the waiting area or the GP's room, although there are a number of rooms to choose from . . . Other services are never suggested and as I do not have access to leaflets and posters around the waiting room I simply do not know they exist . . .' A blind woman interviewed when piloting the questionnaire talked about how exclusive use of print materials not only denies access to basic information, but also infringes the right to privacy.

There are things I wouldn't want to share with my friends about my various bits of medical history and current treatment, but I can't get access to those because they're not made accessible to me privately. I have to quite publicly have information made accessible to me . . . She (GP) has occasionally given me leaflets about things or information and I've had to get someone else to read them . . . Someone else always has to be involved in anything that's written down . . . The doctor writes to me in print the whole time. I've told them before that if they're going to write to me

would they please ring me and tell me as well. The Gas
Board manage to do it, I don't see why the doctor can't.

Issues around privacy and access to information were also
raised by Deaf women and women with learning difficulties.
The lack of qualified sign language interpreters in primary
health care teams often means that Deaf women are dependent on family, friends or children if they need to
communicate with their GP. Whilst Deaf women may find this
wholly unacceptable there is often very little choice and
consequently Deaf women are not likely to gain access to
health care and treatment without having to involve a third
party. Although the use of informal networks such as family
and friends have to some extent been recognised as an
inappropriate method of communicating with non-disabled
women who do not speak English, the parallel lessons have not
been drawn out in relation to Deaf women. Concerns about
privacy and confidentiality may deter Deaf women from
consulting their GP unless it is absolutely necessary. For
example, young Deaf women seeking contraception may not
want to divulge such information to a GP without having the
security of a qualified sign language interpreter who has to
abide by a strict code of ethics.

Women with learning difficulties not only have to battle
with the inaccessibility of print information, but often encounter difficulties with the language used by GPs when
communicating with patients. While communication barriers
constructed by the medical profession are by no means a
problem unique to women with learning difficulties, nevertheless women with learning difficulties often have specific
communication and support needs which are not usually
recognised. Moreover, a general reluctance on the part of
medical professionals to recognise the right of women with
learning difficulties to make decisions and choices about their
lives, means that often there is a tendency to rely on the views
and opinions of parents, carers or other professionals. Consequently there is very little attempt to support women with
learning difficulties and communicate in a straightforward
accessible way which enables them to make decisions about

advice or treatment being offered. The access barriers created by a failure to communicate effectively are particularly significant if women with learning difficulties have no independent support or advocate available to them.

Attitudinal Barriers

People with learning difficulties in particular, but disabled people in general, are often perceived as 'eternal children' and this attitude sometimes influences the way doctors treat us. Victoria talks about her experience:

> Even though he knew I was going to university he still treated me like a child. Once when I was undressing prior to an examination I shouted answers over the screen to questions directed at my mother, which should have been directed at me. I was accused of being cheeky!

Jo wrote how as a child, tinnitus and its upsetting effects were ignored. 'I even had a spurious diagnosis of schizophrenia made due to the assumption that as I was "backward" I would not know the difference between a noise or a voice in my ears.'

Disabled women often find that information is withheld from them. Micheline explains how her GP infringed her privacy by divulging confidential information to her husband. 'I wasn't told I had MS for two years and then I was told because [I asked] "is it MS?" My husband knew two years before I did. I should have been told.' Indeed, GPs sometimes seem to find it easier to communicate through family members (or other acquaintances) than with disabled women directly. Another woman questions whether GPs are naturally uneasy with disabled people '. . . they always seem nervous when sitting in the room . . . they seem uneasy when talking to me, maybe they are naturally nervous!'

It was clear from this survey that disabled women commonly find that a GP's reaction to impairment gets in the way of responding to health care needs. As Eve wrote, 'Sometimes I find that a GP – particularly one who is only here for a short tiime and fairly new – is more interested in my sight problem, or my child's sight problem, than in what I've come to ask about.' And Rachel said, 'It seems that once I mention I have disabilities *all* doctors want to tell me my latest worry is due to these disabilities without even examining me or doing any checking up.'

Some respondents said that they wished their GP would see them more as a whole person, instead of – as KC put it – 'purely as a person with symptoms, no support or under-standing – from a medical perspective only.'

Discriminatory attitudes and assumptions that disabled people inevitably experience a poor quality of life are common throughout our society. There is no reason to assume that GPs will not internalise the prevailing attitudes and this will have a profound effect on the way a doctor responds to a disabled woman's needs. Sally wrote about how damaging this can be:

Family GP who I saw in teens and early twenties most negative, had known me throughout childhood and had very low expectations . . . I tried to cope secretly with incontinence – no support at all from GP. When I asked for help (after support of other spinal cord injured women I met), told to obtain continence supplies 'out of town' – to avoid bringing shame to family.

Negative attitudes held by their doctors will not only affect disabled women's view of themselves but will also result in restrictions on their access to information and health care. Sometimes this will have a profound effect on disabled women's ability to make choices about matters related to their health, and about other areas of their lives such as sexual relationships and whether to have children.

A number of women expressed a feeling that they have to behave in certain ways in order to gain, or retain, support from a GP. Judith wrote of her contrasting experiences of a locum and her own doctor in these terms:

I saw a locum last time who was wonderful – had I applied for this, that, the other? But with my GP, I'll go to her if necessary and she's sort of co-operated to date but there's always this (not always spoken) threat that if I don't comply with treatment she suggests (hospitals, physio, walking) she might withdraw support next time. And this is often for treatments I know could land me in bed for weeks/months on end.

Sometimes the attitudinal barriers created by doctors are those experienced equally by non-disabled people. Elizabeth wrote of her GP 'I find it difficult to talk easily to him – he is a man of very few words and strongly held and orthodox medical opinions.' Monica regrets 'I have always found it difficult to speak to my GP. I am always aware of the small amount of time available . . . I felt he was reluctant to be honest and direct.' While Rosina says, 'She is always in a hurry and is rather dismissive and abrupt.'

Positive experiences

Those women who had good experiences of GPs illustrate how important this can be to them. Most of them emphasised the GP's attitude and the effect this has on both the quality of the service given and on how the woman feels about herself.

Anna, for example, talked about how her GP takes time to understand her needs: 'Although she is very busy her attitude towards me is very friendly, co-operative, understanding. When I first joined the practice I was very ill. She wouldn't let me leave the surgery till she found out what was wrong . . . I was told to call her on any occasion if I was worried'. And Ann said: 'My GP gives me some positive feelings about myself by taking an interest . . . he is a pleasant man who is able to reassure me when I get anxious. He thanks me for making the effort to get to the surgery, so I do not get the feeling of being a nuisance as some disabled people are made to feel.'

Some respondents wrote in terms which indicated that they had fairly low expectations of their doctor and were appreciative of a fairly minimal level of understanding. Joni wrote 'On the whole my GP does try to help me when he can. He is friendly and knows me well. I sometimes just feel that no one is on my side, no one is pushing for me to get a proper diagnosis or any help. He will refer me if I ask him and he always lets me know results of tests and when he's had a letter from the hospital.'

On the other hand, some women received a good quality service. KC explained the importance of her GP's attitude: 'My GP is an extremely effective doctor, who has an under-standing of the needs of disabled women, aside from the medical issues. She is sensitive and open and always willing to make suggestions or to discuss how I feel about a certain area of treatment . . . She is always open to any information with regard to disability issues.' Other women stressed the im-portance of a GP not assuming that all health problems are connected to impairment. Louise wrote 'For the first time, I feel as if I am treated most of the time as if I was a woman and that sometimes my impairment is important and at other times it does not affect my general health.'

GPs were appreciated by women when they communicated well, were able to show empathy, and prescribed or referred on in a way which was felt to be helpful. Judy wrote 'Generally he is *available*, there is no "you only have five minutes and I am already writing out a prescription.' He always turns his chair round so that he is facing you and just *listens*.'

In particular, women appreciate when doctors work in partnership with them, as Fille wrote: 'He has never hesitated to ask my opinions or feelings with regard to the type of treatment or drugs (and their effects) with which he has attempted to treat my problems. I have a particular problem with regard to the usual type of drugs with which to treat osteo-arthritis, allergic to all of them. We usually work as a team to try and find the best alternatives.'

Sally's doctor initiated a record system to promote comm-unication between GP and patient. This meant that 'patients have their own medical CV drawn up from their records – medical backgrounds, operations, medication and personal care needs – one copy kept at the surgery and one held by the patient (updated as necessary) and signed by the GP. Ex-tremely useful if going into hospital or respite care – or if for any reason you are unable to communicate (after an accident, etc.)' This particular GP not only keeps Sally informed by photocopying relevant articles from medical journals for her but was willing to recognise her own lack of knowledge and act on it: 'She attended a training course relating to my impairment, as she had no previous experience in this area, to help her understand my requirements more.'

GP's responses to impairment

It is apparent that a GP's response to a woman's impairment can have a significant impact on her experience of primary health care. About 60 per cent of respondents said that their current doctor responded well to their needs relating to impairment but this left 4 out of 10 women expressing dissatisfaction.

The way GPs reacted to the women's impairments varied greatly. Sometimes the fact that a woman had a condition which the GP did not come across in his/her everyday work meant they responded to women with curiosity and, perhaps, enthusiasm. Phillipa wrote about how her GP 'treated me like a set of interesting symptoms becoming almost excited when presented with symptoms – a "rare case"!' Some women were lucky enough to have a GP who was interested in learning about conditions that they knew little about; others felt that ignorance led to panic. As Jane wrote: 'There is a bit of "panic reaction" in some instances as they feel perhaps their knowledge of my condition is limited. This means that sometimes they may refer me inappropriately to a consultant neurologist when the "problem" is not in that area and either they could treat it themselves or a different speciality would be more appropriate.'

Rosina wrote of the different ways that GPs respond to a lack of knowledge about impairment: 'Some had never even heard of my condition let alone studied anything to do with it. Some, of course, were generally nicer people than others, so this lack of knowledge . . . was easier to take in some cases. Any genuine misunderstanding or not coming across a certain condition before is tolerated when the doctor is a nice person, who does want to help.'

Clearly GPs cannot have a detailed knowledge about all impairments and their effects. However, an ability to find out about women's impairments directly from the women concerned, and a willingness to follow up other sources of information was very important in determining a GP's ability to respond to women's needs. As Izzy wrote: 'He had agreed that we needed a full medical analysis of this impairment and definitive breakdown of the problems and long-term prognosis. He has worked very hard to achieve this and upon receiving this has been reassuring and fairly supportive.'

A GP's personal experience or interest in a particular impairment can sometimes have a big impact on the way a GP interacts with a disabled woman. Penny wrote, for example: 'We share a mutual respect and openness. Since her own mother has developed MS we have exchanged views and medical articles on it – in both directions. I feel most fortunate to have an excellent relationship with her . . .' And Judith said 'I've only once met a GP who believed me (that being more important than any intervention) and that was because her own niece had ME and she'd seen the results for herself.'

Judith wrote of how other GPs had refused to believe her physical symptoms: 'If I don't get well they say it's psychological (hypochondria, etc). If it's psychological it's not real/"genuine" (apparently). If it's not real, it doesn't need treatment. If it doesn't need treatment, it's a sign I just need to "pull myself together". If I argue/disagree/don't comply it's "proof" of these theories. It's a no-win situation regardless of whether it's physical or psychological. They know almost nothing about my situation and seem to feel that's *my inadequacy.*' In contrast, Elizabeth wrote 'My GP believed from the start that I had a genuine physical illness which was serious, he diagnosed ME and referred me on . . . In this respect I have been very lucky.'

Unfortunately, it seems that women with ME and those with conditions such as multiple sclerosis which are sometimes difficult to diagnose are particularly likely to find that their GPs assume that their physical symptoms are rooted in 'psychological' difficulties. As Ruth wrote: 'Everything was put down to nerves – "pull yourself together, there is nothing wrong with you" – during early days before diagnosis.' And Jennifer found that 'as my disability was said to be psychosomatic other illnesses were also blamed on my "mind".' This included a broken wrist which went undiagnosed for two weeks.

As described earlier a number of women wrote about how all health problems tend to be attributed to their impairment. As Micheline wrote: 'Whatever is wrong is due to MS' and Izzy confirmed 'He tends to associate other illnesses as an extension of the main one.' Sharon says that 'Although my lack of sight has nothing to do with, for example, a cold or what contraceptive I take, it is rare that I leave the surgery without some comment being made about it.' On the other hand, Elizabeth appreciated that her GP 'has known me before I had ME and he treats any new complaint seriously not assuming it is just part and parcel of the ME.'

Doctors' ability to identify or empathise with the concerns of disabled women can be an important factor in these women's relationships with GPs. However, as disabled women appear to be marginalised in work on women's health services, and in feminist thinking in general, there is no reason to suggest that they will be better off with a woman GP. Amongst this survey's respondents there were those with poor experiences of female GPs and those with good experiences of male GPs. The most important factors determining such experiences are those of believing what women say about their own health and bodies, and acknowledging their expertise. As Wislocka wrote: 'She is very open and supportive of anything I think may be useful – when I am stuck she asks what I think may be useful first – what I have tried, what I found useful. When I have tried a service e.g. pain clinic, she asks for my evaluation of them – and then suggests how the weak areas could be addressed. When she is lost for an answer she is honest and says she does not know what to do for help.' While, on the other hand, Izzy's experience of a female GP was a negative one: '. . . she tried to get me admitted to the psychiatric hospital twice on the grounds that I was a hysteric/suicide case. I was having an arthritis flare-up on both occasions . . .'

Another issue which merits further research is whether GPs' responses to impairment are influenced by whether the condition is acquired in adulthood or is evident from birth or early childhood. Certainly, within this sample, there were notable differences in women's experiences: those who had been impaired since birth or early childhood reported lower levels of satisfaction with the way their GPs dealt with their needs arising from impairment compared to those who had an acquired impairment.

GPs' responses to disabled women's health care needs as women

There is also a significant difference in women's reported experience of how well GPs respond to their health care needs as women according to whether they have an acquired impairment or not: women who grew up with their impairment reported a lower level of satisfaction with their GPs' response in this area. Further research on doctors' attitudes may highlight whether women who enter adulthood already disabled find that they are less likely to be treated as women. This was certainly Sharon's experience: 'I feel that in general my GPs have viewed me firstly as a blind woman rather than a woman. This has meant that they have not given me the information I have often needed.'

She goes on to highlight the lengths to which her GP went to exert influence over what was 'acceptable' or 'unacceptable' for a disabled woman, the over-riding message being that a blind woman should not have children:

When I was pregnant with my first son I received a letter from the hospital asking me to attend the out-patients at a clinic. I had no idea what it was about, but assumed it was a check-up of some sort. When I arrived I was told that a letter had been sent by someone (whose name could not be divulged), who had suggested that I should be offered an abortion. I was unable to ascertain who had written the letter but at this early stage only my GP knew I was pregnant.

Sharon echoed a number of disabled women's experience when she wrote: 'I have felt on each of my pregnancies ... that I have been viewed as rather a freak. I was made to feel as if I was irresponsible and a cause for concern or that I was wonderful and an inspiration. I do not welcome either label.'

Disabled women's right to have children has been attacked from many quarters yet feminist debates about genetic 'engineering' or abortion have rarely taken on board the reality that women who have physical, sensory or intellectual impairments confront. Sally, who described her impairment as a spinal cord injury resulting from a childhood tumour, wrote

> GP refused to refer me to gynaecologist when I wanted to marry. Refused to prescribe the pill – advised me to obtain sterilisation privately – which I did – reluctantly. Feel very bitter as other women with my impairment have had support and encouragement to have children. Did not know I had the right to change doctor then or had any other choices.

Occasionally a GP was supportive in terms of enabling a disabled woman to choose whether or not to become a mother. Wislocka wrote:

> Despite my back injury I am desperate to have a child. Everyone said I was crazy but my GP looked at it from both sides saying that there may be problems but if I was happy with being a mother I would feel less stressed and may feel less pain. She suggested a referral to someone who does couple counselling about fertility issues and also referred my husband for reversal of vasectomy.

Some women wrote of their experiences of cervical and breast screening in positive terms. Beverley, for example, said that her GP's response in these areas was 'Excellent. When I undergo cervical screening it is difficult for me to be examined in the conventional manner so I am examined lying on my left side. With much patience, time and understanding, nothing is too much trouble.'

On the other hand, Rosina said 'I have difficulty with cervical smear tests and other gynaecological matters as I cannot use an examination couch, and she is reluctant to treat me at home. She does usually agree that I have the smear test done at home but I rather had to plead and justify the reasons I need this. My cervical smear test was due recently. This time my GP has refused to do the test at home and doesn't know where I can get it done. I await an answer from her.' While some GPs obviously give some thought to overcoming difficulties created by mobility impairments, others carry on their practice as if no one will have any difficulty using examination couches whose height is dictated by what is convenient for the examining doctor or nurse rather than the needs of the patient. GPs and women alike would benefit from the dissemination of good practice by doctors who develop new ways of doing things which are based on what disabled women need.

Some respondents indicated that their GP had not offered cervical or breast screening and for Judith this only confirmed her own feelings of genderlessness. 'Am I a woman?' she wrote. 'I lose track most of the time. I never raise these issues with my GP. She doesn't want me to either . . . I don't want to make a fuss in case it confirms their opinion of my "hypochondria"; but most of all I think it's that I don't think of myself often as a "real woman". Interestingly, getting a breast lump was quite a positive experience; *and* my GP at the time treated me as a grown-up, responsible and sexual!! A new experience.'

How a doctor views her/his patient will have a crucial impact on the experience of health care. One woman, in her response to the questions about how well her health care needs as a woman were met, wrote: 'I did not like him writing in my notes "pale, fat, depressed . . ." [He] put me down.' KC, on the other hand, wrote in positive terms of her experiences in this area of health care, saying that her GP had an 'excellent attitude to my self identity as a disabled lesbian'. Further research is needed on how doctors acquire their attitudes to disabled women and how initial and in-service training could help to create better relationships.

Overall, one in five respondents in this sample said that

their current GP did not respond very well, if at all, to their health care needs as women.

Improving disabled women's access to general practitioner services

Many of the women who participated in this research had clear ideas on how their experiences of primary health care could be improved and their needs more appropriately met. Communication, information and a recognition of disabled women's expertise in their own health needs were identified as key factors in ensuring that the contact between disabled women and GPs is constructive.

Sharon explains, 'I think she/he . . . should give me more information about the services they provide. It would also be helpful if the reception staff were more aware of things such as . . . the correct way to lead a blind person.' Clare suggests that her GP could respond to her requirements more appropriately by 'allowing me more control over my health, for example with pain control', while Kate feels that a more constructive approach would be:

> . . . an investigative outlook, more discussion of treatment and prognosis with the patient as an intelligent being whose involvement in solving the problem was desirable.

Judith points out that her GP needs to: 'listen; acknowledge my expertise; acknowledge my experience; acknowledging her lack of expertise and experience'. She goes on to explain:

> I'm not asking for cure . . . I'm asking for support in *managing my situation*. This might mean acknowledging it's tough, helping me access resources, help me plan health management and learn relevant skills.

Maggie makes a number of suggestions for improving disabled women's experience of GPs. She writes: 'I am not prepared to hand over control of any aspect of my life and would wish to take more responsibility for managing my condition. I would like to see:

- accessible surgeries
- patient held records
- administrative structures which are for the patients rather than the staff
- equal opportunities training for all staff
- up to date, easily available information
- a named individual with responsibility for disability issues
- a more extensive primary care team who could respond more quickly to need.'

Conclusion

Many of the issues raised by this research have also been identified by research which focuses on the experience of non-disabled women. The evidence here also indicates, however, that impairment and disability are determining factors in women's access to primary health care.

Impairment in itself creates particular needs which GPs are not always able to recognise or respond to appropriately. Disability – the barriers which deny opportunities to people with impairments – is also a key part of the experience of primary health care in that both physical, communication and attitudinal barriers can impede access to the services women require.

GPs often play a significant role in the lives of disabled women, yet there is very little appreciation of the relationship between impairment, illness and disabled women's health care needs as women. Any future research on women's experience of health care, particularly research informed by a feminist perspective, must incorporate the concerns identified by the women who participated in this research. It is also important that the disabled people's movement takes up access to health care as a campaigning issue. In doing this we must not collude with the medicalisation of our needs and our lives but confront, on our terms, the experience of impairment, insisting that health care needs which are associated with impairment, as well as those which are not, are addressed in ways which empower rather than diminish us.

References

Lloyd, Margaret (1992) 'Does She Boil Eggs? Towards a feminist model of disability', in *Disability Handicap and Society*, Vol. 7, No. 3, pp. 207–21.

Matthews, Gwyneth Ferguson (1983) *Voices from the Shadows*, The Women's Press, Ontario, Canada.

Morris, Jenny, ed. (1989) *Able Lives: Women's Experience of Paralysis*, The Women's Press.

Morris, Jenny (1994) 'Gender and disability', in French, Sally, ed., *On Equal Terms: Working with disabled people*, Butterworth Heinemann.

Oliver, Michael (1992) 'Changing the social relations of research production?' in *Disability Handicap and Society*, Vol. 7, No. 2, pp. 101–14.

Office of Population Censuses and Surveys (1988) *The Prevalence of Disability Among Adults*, HMSO.

Roberts, Helen (1985) *The Patient Patients*, Pandora Press.

CHAPTER NINE

OUT OF ORDER:
Madness is a Feminist and a Disability Issue

Julie McNamara

Madness is a women's issue

Over the last 20 years or so, feminist research has highlighted the way we have inherited a male-defined culture of normality and deviance that defines women as mad by virtue of our gender. The rationale of ordinary behaviour, of what is in order, immediately places women as out of order simply for being female. The idea that women have a propensity for madness goes far beyond the well-researched evidence that women are over-represented in mental institutions and other mental health services. It is an idea that disempowers women who deviate from their expected social role. It isn't sufficient to suggest that the large numbers of women referred to the psychiatric services, or identified as presenting to their GPs with mental distress, are in the grip of their biology. Neither can it be adequately accounted for by focusing on the social conditions of women. The equation is deeply embedded in the cultural archetypes of the Western psyche: to be a woman in our society is to be at risk of being labelled as mad.

Narrow stereotypes of femininity focus on passivity, frailty and dependence; child-like attributes that are at odds with accepted notions of adulthood and maturity. In contrast, the stereotypes of masculinity emphasise competence, activity, analytical ability and independence; all desirable and, above all, adult attributes. Research by feminist psychologists has highlighted the way that the stereotypes of the healthy adult, against which professionals evaluate and diagnose mental distress, conform to the internalised stereotype of the adult male (Broverman *et al.*, 1970; Chesler, 1972; Millett 1991; Ussher, 1993).

Women are generally perceived as unpredictable and unruly victims of our hormones, as neurotic, over-emotional beings. We represent a threat to men and must be brought to order, so we are treated like dirt: 'like matter out of place, that flouts the order of our lives' (Douglas, 1966, p. 2). Those of us who challenge the status quo, step out of role and defy the social constraints that repress our being in the world, become like Phyllis Chesler's 'heroic rebels . . . in an intense experience of female biological, sexual and cultural castration, on a doomed search for potency' (Chesler, 1972, p. 31). Our insanity is as much a 'penalty for being "female" as well as desiring or daring not to be' (p. 16). In a male-dominated society, women are at odds with those in power and are perceived as 'other', or 'not like us'. To be perceived as part of an alien group is to possess 'shameful differentness' (Goffman, 1968, p. 167). To be different, or cast aside as different, is to be 'at risk of falling into madness, or at least to be at risk of being ascribed the label' (Ussher, 1993, p. 140).

Carers who kill: the ultimate horror

Some of the current images of women in the media illustrate how deeply threatening we are in the minds of men. This is evident, for example, in the genre of Madwomen movies which has become something of a cult in recent years. We've had the like of *Fatal Attraction*, *The Hand that Rocks the Cradle*, and *Misery*. The latter two are fascinating as they focus on mad women as nurturers – carers who kill. In each of these movies, women are depicted as harbouring great evil beneath a façade of love and care. It is interesting how powerful women are at the depths of male fantasies. To them we are an unknown quantity on whom they are largely dependent for their nurturing. Their dependency makes them vulnerable and breeds resentment and fear. So what could be more frightening to a man than a woman who defies expectations and does exactly as she feels, when she feels? She becomes uncontrollable, out of order, a Madwoman who renders men impotent.

Misery, in particular, is a masterly exponent of misogyny brewed in castration fears. Here we have a film about a woman who lives alone and therefore outside the bounds of male control. The protagonist, the 'Dragon Lady', is an ex-nurse with a penchant for killing babies and an obsessive fixation on her hero novelist who she rescues in a storm. She hauls him over her shoulder, takes him home and straps him to the bed to nurse him back to health. There she begins killing him with kindness. The wounded man is rendered completely helpless, emasculated by this evil woman, so he sets out to destroy her. There were times when I sympathised with him, when I wanted to spare him – such as when she breaks his ankles yet again for being naughty. However, I could not quite engage with the fantasy of William Goldman, the film-maker, and Stephen King, the writer, of woman as irredeemably evil. At the climax of the battle the hero screams at her, 'You crazy bitch . . . You sick twisted Fuck!' as he finally kills her in an orgiastic frenzy. She dies prostrate on top of him. (It would seem some men are completely phobic about women on top.)

Work by those such as Elaine Showalter (Showalter, 1987) has placed the social construction of madness firmly on the feminist agenda, pointing to psychiatric treatments as an insidious way of subordinating women. But the social construction of madness is also about the policing and control of those people – women *and* men – who do not conform.

Madness is a disability issue

We all harbour prejudices towards differentness or towards those we place as other, whom we set apart from our group. People who experience, and exhibit, mental distress are usually more vulnerable and provide an easy target to scapegoat. Scapegoats are important because they preserve the authority of the establishment who can 'maintain power over those accorded the stigmatised role' (Goffman, 1968, p. 164). Consecutive governments in our industrial age have ensured that people with mental distress, once identified, are segregated from the rest of society. Hence the introduction of coercive legislation from the 1828 and 1845 Asylum Acts through to the 1983 Mental Health Act. Those who do not play their designated social role are re-conditioned or re-programmed to behave in a manner deemed fitting by our guardians of social control: psychiatrists, psychologists and the like (Ussher, 1993, p. 67 and 135; Goffman, 1968, p. 165; Showalter, 1987, p. 137; Foucault, 1979, pp. 146–7).

Western culture places so much emphasis on being in control, on everything being in order and conforming to the current norms that to admit to using mental health services is to admit to being out of order, out of control or mad. In a ferociously capitalist society bent on productivity and consumerism, the principal ethos is survival of the fittest, and anyone who cannot keep up is deemed in-valid – a non-productive failure and a burden on the state.

Once someone has been identified as dysfunctional via the psychiatric services, he or she acquires a psychiatric record and is then denied access to power by being placed as mad, as outside the in group (Ussher, 1993, p. 136). The mental health institutions of this country are swollen with people deemed outsiders by those in control, that is those people with 'labelled violations of social norms' (Scheff, 1966, p. 25). Nowhere else in society are black people and Irish people, women of all classes, lesbians and gays better represented (Ussher, 1993, pp. 138–40; *Race and Class*, 1983).

Let's set aside for the moment the on-going debates on whether mental distress constitutes an impairment or not, whether it is organic or entirely socially constructed. Such debates serve only to divide us from each other, but keep the psychiatric services in employment at least. Deconstructing categories does little for those of us in psychic pain and often denies or distracts from people's actual experiences and the reality of their lives.

It is society that disables people. It is the combination of personal and institutionalized prejudices that create disabling environments. People who have been through the mental health systems or have otherwise acquired a psychiatric history often find their access to employment, housing and other necessities to a good quality life barred by others' subtle and not-so-subtle discriminatory behaviour. People with mental distress are disabled. Disability is about removing people's power, or denying access to power. Those who use the mental health system are disabled by the enormity of societal and personal prejudices directed at us. It thus becomes clear why the Disability Movement must include survivors of the mental health system.

Survivor, or mental health system survivor, are terms coined by the radical campaigning group, Survivors Speak Out which originated at the Mental Health 2000 Conference held in Brighton in 1985. The group is made up of survivors of the psychiatric and psychological services in this country and campaigns for better treatment of people who have been diagnosed mentally ill and towards the restoration of our basic human rights. Survivor is a term which I embrace with pride because it speaks of hope beyond despair, an existence in spite of life's traumas and, often, in spite of treatment received within the mental health services. It is also a term which inflames the sensibilities of the majority of those working in the psychiatric profession.

Disabled people have, until recently, tended to want to distance themselves from the Survivors Movement. Unfortunately, prejudice can be as rife within the disability movement as it is outside it and we experience the age-old stigma that attaches itself to people with mental distress. Morever, there sometimes seems to be a hierarchy of oppression within the movement, with people with 'hidden impairments' treated with suspicion. For some people, we are far too symmetrical in physique to be included. Thankfully, both these kinds of excluding attitudes are beginning to shift and it was heartening that so many psychiatric survivors joined, and were welcomed on, the civil rights demonstrations during 1994.

The personal is political

Let's look at what actually happens to somebody in mental distress. The allegedly ill person is in a sense accused, then restrained and segregated from society. In some instances they are locked up and detained against their will, and sometimes 'offered' electro-torture of the brain in the guise of therapy. Kate Millett describes her own experiences of the traditional psychiatric regime as 'the terrorism of the state against the individual' (Millett 1991, p. 10). When faced with enforced incarceration by the powers that be, paranoia is a healthy response.

The mental health system is modelled on that of the penal system with one crucial difference – within the penal system, most convictions are 'spent', that is erased from the records after five years. In the case of the mental health system, on the other hand, your history will follow you around in your medical records for the rest of your life. Having a psychiatric history means that certain professions are closed to you, and you will have difficulty getting insurance, fostering or adopting children and obtaining a visa to visit certain countries. This can have far-reaching effects, as I have learned at great cost over the years.

Early in September 1983, after three years of psycho-therapeutic treatment, being transferred from one clinic to another, I was discharged as an out-patient from St Anne's Hospital, Nottingham. Two years later I lost a job I was offered as a residential social worker in St Albans. On the day I was due to begin work I received a letter, delivered by hand, telling me that my application for the post had been 'un-successful'. That letter contradicted a previous one 'de-lighting' in my 'successful application' and inviting me to meet the staff and residents at the house; we had established my duty rota long before the start date.

I decided to ignore the second letter and challenged their concept of reality by turning up for work, armed with the original letter. I was turned away.

The reason was that I had failed a medical I had never been invited to attend, neither by my own GP who knew little about me since I had only recently signed up with his practice, nor by the medical personnel of the social services department I was joining. My enquiries revealed that I had been written off on the basis of the psychiatric history recorded in my medical file. The GP and the medical officer of the social services department had described me as 'fundamentally emotionally unstable and unfit for such work'. 'Such work' was located at a mental health rehabilitation project. If these two male medics had decided that I was unfit for such work in the community, then perhaps they were saying that it is not possible to rehabilitate psychiatric patients, current or past. If that was the case, why waste all that public money on the project?

It was a dirty fight and since I had nothing to lose, I went public all the way. I called upon the help of the local Labour Party, the National Council for Civil Liberties (now Liberty) and, of course, the press. Seven months later, I was offered my job back with a full apology from the Director of Social Services for the 'administrative error' that had meant I wasn't invited to attend my own medical examination. Apparently, it is possible to rehabilitate people after all. Until government regulations passed in 1991 it was not possible to gain access to medical records, which are effectively the property of the Secretary of State. However, by threatening the GP concerned with a negligence suit I was allowed to see the contents of mine. I was not able to challenge what was written there, but at least I know now what I'm up against from the creative writing exercises of a variety of professionals who have spent little more than 20 minutes apiece interviewing me but whose words will disable me for the rest of my life.

My story is not at all unusual. In the context of a male-dominated society, women's voices are stifled and silenced at every level. We are dismissed as hysterical at the best of times, but women who have been diagnosed within the psychiatric services stand little chance of being taken seriously. We are on the receiving end of disabling and sexist interpretations of our life experiences.

A caring community?
Our welfare system is being disassembled and auctioned off before our eyes. We are being sold the myth of a new caring community where, with all our vulnerabilities, we will be nurtured in love and succour. The major long-stay hospitals for 'subnormality' and the big 'bins' in psychiatry have been decanted over the past 30 years and yet there are still 90 large

psychiatric hospitals open in England out of 130 recorded in the 1960s (Sayce, 1994, pp. 4–5). And the resources in the community are miserably inadequate, as MIND and other organisations have consistently pointed out. There are too few crisis houses or therapeutic communities which means there is little choice of treatment for people in distress. It also means that people in distress often have to rely on family or friends to support them in trying to stay out of hospital.

Women represent an overwhelming majority of our unpaid carers, our 'informal carers', bearing the brunt of a callously underfunded government policy. But women care, don't we? We were raised to care. The exploitation of our socialised helpfulness is a cynical abuse of institutionalised sexism (Marshall, 1985, pp. 32–6). Is it any wonder that women are more likely than men to seek help from their GP or present with depression? (Brown and Harris, 1978). We're not mad, we're angry. In fact we're bloody furious.

The current media witch-hunt of survivors of mental health services who are 'at large' in the community is a terrifying crystallisation of society's prejudices towards people in distress. Those who use the psychiatric services are commonly perceived as a violent threat to the community and yet they are a hundred times more dangerous to themselves than to others (Prins, 1990). A small minority of people using mental health services do become violent, usually during a period of disturbance. Sometimes there are tragic results as with the death of Jonathan Zito, killed by Christopher Clunis. This one act may have enormous repercussions for all users of psychiatric services. The Secretary of State for Health reacted by initiating a 10-point plan bringing in tighter controls over the release of 'mentally disordered' people into the community, and greater powers of supervised discharge. This was in response to public outcry stirred up by sensationalised reporting in the press. When we examine how the stigma attached to mental distress is kept alive, journalists have a lot to answer for – one study found that two thirds of all media references to 'mental illness' focused on violence (Philo *et al.*, eds, 1993).

Survivors Speak Out has been working hard at challenging

the stereotypes in the mass media, encouraging survivors to speak for themselves, confronting the myths and quashing the prejudices. But in the meantime government policy has been reinforcing fears in the community towards 'psychiatric patients'. Their 10-point plan describes 'new steps to tighten substantially community care for mentally ill people' (Department of Health, Press Release, 12 August 1994). Initially it was proposed that electronic identity tags should be introduced to monitor the movements of those people who had been 'sectioned' or coerced into treatment. This met with an outcry from users of and practitioners in mental health services alike. It was argued that 'tagging' was barbaric and might be counterproductive in therapeutic terms. Secretary of State Virginia Bottomley backed down but opted for 'the legal sanction that patients who do not comply with their programme of care may be recalled compulsorily to hospital' and the requirement on providers of services to maintain 'supervision registers' of those 'patients most at risk' (Department of Health, Press Release, 24 February 1994). Guidance on the registration and supervision of discharged patients has created the situation where people will be watched by Big Brother for the rest of their lives. I can't see that improving paranoia.

Hackney, the London borough where I live, has the highest number of referrals under Section 136 of the Mental Health Act (police referrals) to mental health systems in the country. The majority of these referrals are young black men between the ages of 18 and 26. Is that about care in the community or the racist policing of a community?

We must have a say

If we look at who is setting the agenda for change at the moment, it is clear that power is still in the hands of non-disabled professionals, the 'specialists' who have devoted their lives to studying the phenomena of 'deviant behaviour'. It is very rare to find a professional who is a survivor of the system or who will admit to experiencing mental distress.

For example, at the 1993 International Women and Mental Health Conference, not one speaker described their own life experiences. Instead, each professional in turn presented their clients' lives before us, like interesting case material open to scrutiny and investigation. This was a feminist conference – run by women who profess to understand power dynamics and how we are made powerless. Yet this was a prime example of the disenfranchisement of mental health system survivors. Feminist psychologists and therapists appropriated other women's experiences. They, like their male professional colleagues, control the lives of women in the mental health system.

The stigma attached to people who are in distress is such that trained professionals or helpers are afraid to admit to emotional vulnerability at all. Women survivors need to be central to all the decision-making processes that create mental health services. Because we are not, we do not have a choice in the help we receive, in how we are treated or where.

The power issues are written large before us. We need to challenge the social forces which create an underclass of people – 'the disabled', those less-than-human beings with less than all their faculties. In turn we need to challenge the culture of guilt-ridden do-gooders muttering 'there but for the grace of God go I' as they yank the nearest blind woman across a road they'd no intention of crossing and repossess the next group of disabled women to fill their empty sunshine coaches.

It is crucial that women survivors are present in the disabled people's movement. We need to create coalitions of disabled people and survivors to fight for civil rights, for survival. We also need coalitions to make positive changes in a world which has created a false divide between those who purchase and provide treatment and those who receive it. As Bernice Johnson Reagon points out, 'coalition work is not done in your home. Coalition work has to be done in the streets . . . it is the most dangerous work you can do and you shouldn't look for comfort . . . I ain't gonna let you live unless you let me live' (Johnson Reagon, 1985). It may feel uncomfortable for women psychologists and therapists to give up the aura of mystique and the taste of power and allow women survivors to take control of their own destinies. It may hurt to give up the ladder of power in the disabled people's movement between those with visible and those with 'hidden' impairments. Within the survivors movement it will mean healing the rifts between women who have survived psychiatric treatment and women who pay for therapy. Unless we can be honest about our differences and our fear of difference then we cannot work together and we cannot change the world.

References

Broverman, K. *et al.* (1970) 'Sex role stereotypes and clinical judgements of mental health', in *Journal of Consulting and Clinical Psychology*, 34, 1, pp. 1–7.

Brown, G. W. and Harris, T. (1978) *Social Origins of Depression: A study of psychiatric disorder in women*, Tavistock.

Chesler, Phyllis (1972) *Women and Madness*, Avon Books.

Department of Health (1994) *Health Secretary Announces New Monitoring Arrangements*, Press Release, 24 February.

Department of Health (1994) *Legislation Planned to Provide for Supervised Discharge of Psychiatric Patients*, Press Release, 12 August.

Douglas, Mary (1966) *Purity and Danger: An analysis of the concepts of pollution and taboo*, Routledge.

Goffman, Erving (1968) *Stigma: Notes on the management of a spoiled identity*, Pelican.

Foucault, M. (1979) *The History of Sexuality: An introduction*, Allen Lane.

Johnson Reagon, Bernice (1985) 'Coalition Politics: turning the century', in *Trouble and Strife*, 6, Summer, pp. 30–5.

Marshall, Kate (1985) *Moral Panics and Victorian Values: Women and the family in Thatcher's Britain*, Revolutionary Communist Party/Jurious.

Millett, Kate (1991) *The Loony Bin Trip*, Virago.

Prins, H. (1990) 'Dangerousness: A review' in Bluglass R. and Bowden, P., eds., *Principles and Practice of Forensic Psychiatry*, Longman.

Race and Class (1983) 'Psychiatry and the Corporate State', Vol. 25, No. 2.

Sayce, Liz (1994) 'Eight Community Care Myths', in *OpenMind*, No. 68, pp. 4–5.

Scheff, T. J. (1966) *Being Mentally Ill*, Weidenfield and Nicolson.
Showalter, Elaine (1987) *The Female Malady: Women, madness and English culture 1930–1980*, Virago.
Ussher, Jane (1993) *Womens' Madness: Misogyny or mental illness?* Harvester Wheatsheaf.

CHAPTER TEN

INCLUDING ALL OF OUR LIVES:
Renewing the Social Model of Disability
Liz Crow

This chapter has its origins in an article written for Coalition *– one of the journals of the British disabled people's movement. In the four years since it appeared in that initial form, both discussions with other disabled people and my own circumstances have influenced my thinking. During that time, we have started to talk more freely about our experiences of impairment and the more fully developed form of the social model of disability that is advocated here is already beginning to be applied informally within the disabled people's movement.*

My life has two phases: before the social model of disability, and after it. Discovering this way of thinking about my experiences was the proverbial raft in stormy seas. It gave me an understanding of my life, shared with thousands, even millions, of other people around the world, and I clung to it.

This was the explanation I had sought for years. Suddenly what I had always known, deep down, was confirmed. It wasn't my body that was responsible for all my difficulties, it was external factors, the barriers constructed by the society in which I live. I was being dis-abled – my capabilities and opportunities were being restricted – by prejudice, discrimination, inaccessible environments and inadequate support. Even more important, if all the problems had been created by society, then surely society could un-create them. Revolutionary!

For years now this social model of disability has enabled me to confront, survive and even surmount countless situations of exclusion and discrimination. It has been my mainstay, as it has been for the wider disabled people's movement. It has enabled a vision of ourselves free from the constraints of disability (oppression) and provided a direction for our commitment to social change. It has played a central role in promoting disabled people's individual self-worth, collective identity and political organisation. I don't think it is an exaggeration to say that the social model has saved lives. Gradually, very gradually, its sphere is extending beyond our movement to influence policy and practice in the mainstream. The contribution of the social model of disability, now and in the future, to achieving equal rights for disabled people is incalculable.

So how is it that, suddenly to me, for all its strengths and relevance, the social model doesn't seem so water-tight anymore? It is with trepidation that I criticise it. However, when personal experience no longer matches current explanations, then it is time to question afresh.

Disability is 'all'?

The social model of disability has been our key to dismantling the traditional conception of impairment[1] as 'personal tragedy' and the oppression that this creates.

Mainstream explanations have centred on impairment as 'all' – impairment as the cause of our experiences and disadvantage, and impairment as the focus of intervention. The World Health Organisation defines impairment and related concepts as follows:

Impairment: Any loss or abnormality of psychological, physiological, or anatomical structure or function. *Disability*: Any restriction or lack (resulting from impairment) of ability to perform an activity in the manner or within the range considered normal for a human being. *Handicap*: A disadvantage for a given individual, resulting from an impairment or disability, that limits or prevents fulfilment of a role that is normal, depending on age, sex, social or cultural factors for that individual. (United Nations Division for Economic and Social Information, 1983, p. 3)

Within this framework, which is often called the medical model of disability, a person's functional limitations (impairments) are the root cause of any disadvantages experienced and these disadvantages can therefore only be rectified by treatment or cure.

The social model, in contrast, shifts the focus from impairment onto disability, using this term to refer to disabling social, environmental and attitudinal barriers rather than lack of ability. Thus, while impairment is the functional limitation(s) which affect a person's body, disability is the loss or limitation of opportunities resulting from direct and indirect discrimination. Social change – the removal of disabling barriers – is the solution to the disadvantages we experience.

This way of seeing things opens up opportunities for the eradication of prejudice and discrimination. In contrast, the medical model makes the removal of disadvantage contingent upon the removal or 'overcoming' of impairment – full participation in society is only to be found through cure or fortitude. Small wonder, therefore, that we have focused so strongly on the importance of disabling barriers and struggled to dismantle them.

In doing so, however, we have tended to centre on disability as 'all'. Sometimes it feels as if this focus is so absolute that we are in danger of assuming that impairment has no part at all in determining our experiences. Instead of tackling the contradictions and complexities of our experiences head on, we have chosen in our campaigns to present impairment as irrelevant, neutral and, sometimes, positive, but never, ever as the quandary it really is.

Why has impairment been so excluded from our analysis? Do we believe that admitting there could be a difficult side to impairment will undermine the strong, positive (SuperCrip?) images of our campaigns? Or that showing every single problem cannot be solved by social change will inhibit or excuse non-disabled people from tackling anything at all? Or that we may make the issues so complex that people feel constructive change is outside their grasp? Or even that admitting it can sometimes be awful to have impairments may fuel the belief that our lives are not worth living?

Bring back impairment!

The experience of impairment is not always irrelevant, neutral or positive. How can it be when it is the very reason used to justify the oppression we are battling against? How can it be when pain, fatigue, depression and chronic illness are constant facts of life for many of us?

We align ourselves with other civil rights movements and we have learnt much from those campaigns. But we have one fundamental difference from other movements, which we cannot afford to ignore. There is nothing inherently unpleasant or difficult about other groups' embodiment: sexuality, sex and skin colour are neutral facts. In contrast, impairment means our experience of our bodies *can* be unpleasant or difficult. This does not mean our campaigns against disability are any less vital than those against heterosexism, sexism or racism; it does mean that for many disabled people personal struggle related to impairment will remain even when disabling barriers no longer exist.

Yet our insistence that disadvantage and exclusion are the result of discrimination and prejudice, and our criticisms of the medical model of disability, have made us wary of acknowledging our experiences of impairment. Impairment is safer not mentioned at all.

This silence prevents us from dealing effectively with the difficult aspects of impairment. Many of us remain frustrated and disheartened by pain, fatigue, depression and chronic illness, including the way they prevent us from realising our potential or railing fully against disability (our experience of exclusion and discrimination); many of us fear for our futures with progressive or additional impairments; we mourn past activities that are no longer possible for us; we are afraid we may die early or that suicide may seem our only option; we desperately seek some effective medical intervention; we feel ambivalent about the possibilities of our children having impairments; and we are motivated to work for the prevention of impairments. Yet our silence about impairment has made many of these things taboo and created a whole new series of constraints on our self-expression.

Of course, the suppression of concerns related to impairment does not mean they cease to exist or suddenly become more bearable. Instead this silencing undermines individuals' ability to 'cope' and, ultimately, the whole disabled people's movement. As individuals, most of us simply cannot pretend with any conviction that our impairments are irrelevant because they influence so much of our lives. External disabling barriers may create social and economic disadvantage but our subjective experience of our bodies is also an integral part of our everyday reality. What we need is to find a way to integrate impairment into our whole experience and sense of our selves for the sake of our own physical and emotional well-being, and, subsequently, for our individual and collective capacity to work against disability.

As a movement, we need to be informed about disability *and* impairment in all their diversity if our campaigns are to be open to all disabled people. Many people find that it is their experience of their bodies – and not only disabling barriers such as inaccessible public transport – which make political involvement difficult. For example, an individual's capacity to attend meetings and events might be restricted because of limited energy. If these circumstances remain acknowledged, then alternative ways of contributing are unlikely to be sought. If our structures and strategies (i.e. *how* we organise and offer support in our debates, consultation and demonstrations) cannot involve all disabled people, then our campaigns lose the contributions of many people. If our movement excludes many disabled people or refuses to discuss certain issues then our understanding is partial: our collective ability to conceive of, and achieve, a world which does not disable is diminished. What we risk is a world which includes an 'elite' of people with impairments, but which for many more of us contains no real promise of civil rights, equality or belonging. How can we expect anyone to take seriously a 'radical' movement which replicates some of the worst exclusionary aspects of the society it purports to change?

Our current approach to the social model is the ultimate irony: in tackling only one side of our situation we disable ourselves.

Redefining impairment

Our fears about acknowledging the implications of impairment are quite justified. Dominant perceptions of impairment as personal tragedy are regularly used to undermine the work of the disabled people's movement and they rarely coincide with disabled people's understandings of their circumstances. They are individualistic interpretations: our experiences are entirely explained by each individual's psychological or biological characteristics. Any problems we encounter are explained by personal inadequacy or functional limitation, to the exclusion of social influences.

These interpretations impose narrow assumptions about the varying experiences of impairment and isolate experience from its disabling context. They also segregate us from each other and from people without impairments. Interpreting impairment as personal tragedy creates fear of impairment and an emphasis on medical intervention. Such an interpretation is a key part of the attitudes and actions that disable us.

However, the perception of impairment as personal tragedy is merely a social construction; it is not an inevitable way of thinking about impairment. Recognising the importance of impairment for us does not mean that we have to take on the non-disabled world's ways of interpreting our experience of our bodies. In fact, impairment, at its most basic level, is a purely objective concept which carries no intrinsic meaning. Impairment simply means that aspects of a person's body do not function or they function with difficulty. Frequently this is taken a stage further to imply that the person's body, and ultimately the person, is inferior. However, the first is fact; the second is interpretation. If these interpretations are socially created then they are not fixed or inevitable and it is possible to replace them with alternative interpretations based on our own experience of impairment rather than what our impairments mean to non-disabled people.

We need a new approach which acknowledges that people apply their own meanings to their own experiences of impairment. This self-interpretation adds a whole new layer of personal, subjective meanings to the objective concept of impairment. The personal interpretation incorporates any meaning that impairment holds for an individual (ie, any effects it has on their activities), the feelings it produces (eg, pain) and any concerns the individual might have (eg, how their impairment might progress). Individuals might regard their impairment as positive, neutral or negative, and this might differ according to time and changing circumstances.

With this approach the experiences and history of our impairments become a part of our autobiography. They join our experience of disability and other aspects of our lives to form a complete sense of ourselves.

Acknowledging the relevance of impairment is essential to ensuring that people are knowledgeable about their own circumstances. An individual's familiarity with how their body works allows them to identify their specific needs. This is a precursor to meeting those needs by accessing existing information and resources. Self-knowledge is the first stage of empowerment and gives a strong base for individuals to work collectively to confront disability and its impact upon people with impairments.

We need to think about impairment in three, related ways:

- First, there is the objective concept of *impairment*. This was agreed in 1976 by the Union of Physically Impaired Against Segregation (UPIAS, 1976) and has since been developed by Disabled People's International (DPI) to include people with a range of non-physical impairments:

  Impairment: lacking all or part of a limb, or having a defective limb, organism or mechanism of the body.

- Second, there is the individual interpretation of the *subjective experience of impairment* in which an individual binds their own meanings to the concept of impairment to convey their personal circumstances.

- Finally, there is the impact of the wider *social context* upon impairment, in which misrepresentation, social exclusion and discrimination combine to disable people with impairments.

It is this third aspect to impairment which is not inevitable and its removal is the primary focus of the disabled people's movement. However, all three layers are currently essential to an understanding of our personal and social experiences.

Responses to impairment

We need to reclaim and acknowledge our personal experiences of impairment in order to develop our key debates, to incorporate this experience into the wider social context and target any action more precisely. One critical area of concern is the different responses to impairment, for ultimately these determine our exclusion or inclusion.

Currently, the main responses to impairment divide into four broad categories:

- *avoidance/'escape'*, through abortion, sterilisation, withholding treatment from disabled babies, infanticide and euthanasia (medically assisted suicide) or suicide.
- *management*, in which any difficult effects of impairment are minimised and incorporated into our individual lives, without any significant change in the impairment.
- *cure* through medical intervention.
- *prevention* including vaccination, health education and improved social conditions.

The specific treatments that emerge from these responses differ markedly according to whether they are based on the medical or social model. Currently, the treatment available is dominated by the medical model's individualistic interpretation of impairment as tragic and problematic and the sole cause of disadvantage and difficulty. This leads policy-makers and professionals to seek a 'solution' through the removal of impairment. Each of the above responses is considered, at different times and in different contexts, to be valuable in bringing about the perceived desired outcome of reducing the number of people with impairments. The result is often a fundamental undermining of our civil and human rights.

For example, although not currently legal in Britain, euthanasia and infanticide are widely advocated where the 'quality of life' of someone with an impairment is deemed unacceptably low. An increasing number of infanticide and euthanasia cases have reached the courts in recent years, with judgements and public responses implying increasing approval. Infanticide is justified on grounds that 'killing a defective infant is not morally equivalent to killing a person. Very often it is not wrong at all.'[2] Suicide amongst people with impairments is frequently considered far more rational than in people without, as though impairment renders it the obvious, even the only, route to take. Ruth Bailey's chapter has illustrated how assumptions of the inevitable poor quality of life with an impairment dominate the development of prenatal screening and abortion. These approaches have created a huge research industry, and foetal screening and abortion are now major users of impairment-related resources.

Prevention of impairment through public health measures receives only minimal consideration and resourcing. The isolation of impairment from its social context means the social and economic causes of impairment often go unrecognised. The definitions of prevention are also questionable, in that foetal screening and subsequent abortion are categorised by mainstream approaches as preventative, whereas in reality such action is about the elimination of impairment.

Where removal of impairment is not possible, mainstream approaches extend to the management of impairment, although this remains one of the most under-resourced areas of the health service. However, much of the work in this area, rather than increasing an individual's access to and control over the help that they might need, is more about disguising or concealing impairment. Huge amounts of energy and resources are spent by medical and rehabilitation services to achieve this. For example, many individuals are prescribed cosmetic surgery and prostheses which have no practical function and may actually inhibit an individual's use of their body. Others are taught to struggle for hours to dress themselves when the provision of personal assistance would be more effective.

There are a number of critical flaws in mainstream interpretations of impairment and associated responses. First, little distinction is made between different people's experience of impairment or different aspects of a single impairment – or indeed, whether there may be positive aspects to some impairments. Instead, resources are applied in a generalised way to end impairment, regardless of the actual experience and interpretations of the individuals concerned. With the development of genetic screening, intervention aims to eliminate people with specific types of impairment altogether. Rarely is consideration given to the positive attributes of impairment, for example, the cystic fibrosis gene confers resistance to cholera which is an important benefit in some parts of the world. Associations are being identified between some impairments and creative or intellectual talent, while impairment in itself requires the development of more co-operative and communitarian ways of working and living – an advantage in a society with so much conflict to resolve.

Second, impairment is presented as the full explanation, with no recognition of disability. Massive resources are directed into impairment-related research and interventions. In contrast, scant resources are channelled into social change for the inclusion of people with impairments. For example, research will strive to 'cure' an individual of their walking difficulty, whilst ignoring the social factors which make not walking into a problem. There is little public questioning of the distribution of funds between these two approaches. Additionally, such assumptions inhibit many disabled people from recognising the true causes of their circumstances and initiating appropriate responses.

A third criticism is that, while these responses to impairment are seen as representing the interests of disabled people, they are made largely by people with no direct experience of impairment, yet are presented as authoritative. Disabled people's knowledge, in contrast, is frequently derided as emotional and therefore lacking validity.[3] Although main-stream interventions are presented as being for the benefit of disabled people, in fact they are made for a non-disabled society. Ingrained assumptions and official directives make it clear that there is an implicit, and sometimes explicit, intention of population control. Abortion, euthanasia and cure are presented as 'quality of life' issues, but are also justified in terms of economic savings or 'improvement' to populations.[4]

It is counteracting these and related concerns which moti-vates the disabled people's movement. The social model of disability rejects the notion of impairment as problematic, focusing instead on discrimination as the key obstacle to a disabled person's quality of life. The logical extension of this approach is to seek a solution through the removal of disability and this is what the disabled people's movement works towards.

As a result, the overriding emphasis of the movement is on social change to end discrimination against people with impairments. There is a strong resistance to considering impairment as relevant to our political analysis. When im-pairment is discussed at all within the disabled people's movement it tends to be in the context of criticising main-stream responses. We have, for example, clearly stated that foetal screening for abortion and the implicit acceptance of infanticide for babies with significant impairments are based on assumptions that our lives are not worth living. Our intervention in public debates in recent years about medically assisted suicide (euthanasia) has exposed the same assumption. In contrast, we have asserted the value of our lives and the importance of external disabling barriers, rather than im-pairment in itself, in determining quality of life. The same perspective informs our criticisms of the resources spent on attempting to 'cure' people of their impairments.

It is this rejection of impairment as problematic, however, that is the social model's flaw. Although social factors *do* generally dominate in determining experience and quality of life – for example requests for euthanasia are more likely to be motivated by lack of appropriate assistance than pain (Seale and Addington-Hall, 1994) – impairment *is* relevant. For fear of appearing to endorse mainstream responses, we are in danger of failing to acknowledge that for some individuals impairment – as well as disability – causes disadvantage.

Not acknowledging impairment also lays the disabled people's movement open to misappropriation and misinterpretation. For example, disabled people's concerns about genetic screening and euthansia have been used by 'pro-life' groups to strengthen their arguments. Equally, the movement's rejection of medical and rehabilitation professionals' approaches to treatment and cure has not been accompanied by an exploration of what forms of intervention *would* be useful. Our message tends to come across as rejecting all forms of intervention when it is clear that some interventions, such as the alleviation of pain, in fact require more attention and resources. In both cases, the reluctance of the disabled people's movement to address the full implications of impairment leaves its stance ambiguous and open to misuse.

It is also clear that, by refusing to discuss impairment, we are failing to acknowledge the subjective reality of many disabled people's daily lives. Impairment *is* problematic for people who experience pain, illness, shortened lifespan or other factors. As a result, they may seek treatment to minimise these consequences and, in extreme circumstances, may no longer wish to live. It is vital not to assume that they are experiencing a kind of 'false consciousness' – that if all the external disabling barriers were removed they would no longer feel like this. We need to ensure the availability of all the support and resources that an individual might need, whilst acknowledging that impairment *can* still be intolerable.

This does not imply that *all* impairment is intolerable, or that impairment causes *all* related disadvantage; nor does it negate the urgency with which disability must be confronted and removed. It simply allows us, alongside wider social and political change, to recognise people's experiences of their bodies. Without incorporating a renewed approach to impairment we cannot achieve this.

A renewed social model of disability

We need to take a fresh look at the social model of disability and learn to integrate all its complexities. It is critical that we recognise the ways in which disability and impairment work together. The social model has never suggested that disability represents the total explanation or that impairment doesn't count – that has simply been the impression we have given by keeping our experiences of impairment private and failing to incorporate them into our public political analysis.

We need to focus on disability *and* impairment: on the external and internal constituents they bring to our experiences. Impairment is about our bodies' ways of working and any implications these hold for our lives. Disability is about the reaction and impact of the outside world on our particular bodies. One cannot be fully understood without attention to the other, because whilst they can exist independently of each other, there are also circumstances where they interact. And whilst there are common strands to the way they operate, the balance between disability and impairment, their impact and the explanations of their cause and effect will vary according to each individual's situation and from time to time.

We need a renewed social model of disability. This model would operate on two levels: a more complete understanding of disability and impairment as social concepts; and a recognition of an individual's experiences of their body over time and in variable circumstances. This social model of disability is thus a means to encapsulating the total experience of both disability and impairment.

Our current approach is based primarily on the idea that once the struggle against disability is complete, only the impairment will remain for the individual and there will be no disadvantage associated with this. In other words, when disability comes to an end there will be no socially-created barriers to transport, housing, education and so on for people with impairments. Impairment will not then be used as a pretext for excluding people from society. People with impairments will be able to participate in and contribute to society on a par with people who do not have impairments.

In this non-disabling society, however, impairment may well be unaltered and some individuals will find that disadvantages remain. Removal of disability does not necessarily mean the removal of restricted opportunities. For example, limitations to an individual's health and energy levels or their experience of pain may constrain their participation in activities. Impairment *in itself* can be a negative, painful experience.

Moreover, whilst an end to disability means people with impairments will no longer be discriminated against, they may remain disadvantaged in their social and economic opportunities by the long-term effects of earlier discrimination. Although affirmative action is an important factor in alleviating this, it is unlikely to be able to undo the full scale of discrimination for everyone.

Our current interpretation of the social model also tends to assume that if *impairment* ceases, then the individual will no longer experience disability. In practice, however, they may continue to be disabled, albeit to a lesser degree than previously. Future employment opportunities, for example, are likely to be affected by past discrimination in education even when impairment no longer exists.

In addition, an end to impairment may trigger a massive upheaval to those aspects of an individual's self-identity and image formed in response to disability and impairment. It can also signal the loss of what may be an individual's primary community. These personal and collective identities are formed in response to disability. That further changes may be required in changing circumstances is a sign of the continuing legacy of disability.

Our current approach also misses the fact that people can be disabled even when they have no impairment. Genetic and viral testing is now widely used to predict the probability of an individual subsequently acquiring a particular impairment. Fear has been expressed that predisposition to impairment will be used as a basis for discrimination, particularly in financial and medical services.[5]

There are also circumstances in which disability and impairment exist independently, and change in one is not necessarily linked to change in the other. For example, disability can dramatically ease or worsen with changes to an individual's environment or activities even when their particular impairment is static. Leaving a purpose-built home to go on holiday, for example, may give rise to a range of access restrictions not usually encountered, even though an individual's impairment remains the same. Equally, an employee with an impairment may find their capacity to succeed at work is confounded within one organisation but fully possible in another simply because of differences in the organisations' equality practices.

Where level of impairment increases, disability does not necessarily follow suit if adequate and appropriate resources are readily available to meet changes in need. A new impairment, a condition which fluctuates or a progressive impairment may mean that an individual needs additional or changing levels of personal assistance, but disability will remain constant if that resource is easily accessed, appropriate and flexible.

Perhaps most importantly, however, disability and impairment *interact*. Impairment must be present in the first instance for disability to be triggered: disability is the form of discrimination that acts specifically against people with (or who have had) impairments. This does not mean that impairment causes disability, but that it is a precondition for that particular oppression.

However, the difficulties associated with a particular impairment can influence the degree to which disability causes disadvantage. For example, an individual with a chronic illness may have periods in which their contact with the social world is curtailed to such an extent that external restrictions become irrelevant. At times of improved health the balance between impairment and disability may shift, with opportunities lost through discrimination being paramount.

Impairment can also be caused or compounded by disability. An excessively steep ramp, for example, might cause new impairment or exacerbate pain. An inaccessible health centre can restrict the availability of health screening that would otherwise prevent certain impairments, whilst inadequate resourcing can mean that pain reduction or management techniques are not available to many of the people who need them. Medical treatments – including those used primarily for cosmetic purposes – can cause impairment, for example, it has now emerged that a 'side effect' of growth hormone treatment is the fatal Creutzfeldt-Jakob disease.

Discrimination in general can also cause major emotional stress and place mental health at risk. Our reluctance to discuss impairment obscures this aspect of disability. If we present impairment as irrelevant then, even where impairment is caused by disability, it is, by implication, not a problem. This limits our ability to tackle social causes of impairment and so diminishes our campaigns.

Like disability, other experiences of inequality can also create or increase impairment. For example, abuse associated with racism or heterosexism, sexist pressure to modify physical appearance and lack of basic provision because of poverty can all lead to impairment. A significant proportion of people become active in the disabled people's movement as a result of such experiences, or through a recognition of these (and other) links that exist between oppressions.

Different social groups can also experience diverse patterns of impairment for a variety of social and biological reasons. Impairment for women, for example, is more likely to be associated with chronic pain, illness and old age (Morris, 1994, pp. 210–12). Excluding the implications of impairment risks reducing the relevance of the social model of disability to certain social groups. For example, the most common cause of impairment amongst women, is a chronic condition, arthritis, where the major manifestation of impairment is pain. Unless the social model of disability incorporates a recognition of the patterns of impairment experienced by different social groups, there will be a failure to develop appropriate services.

Impairment can also be influenced by other external factors, not necessarily discriminatory, which may be physical, psychological or behavioural. Differences in cultural and individual approaches to pain and illness, for example, can significantly affect the way a person feels, perceives and reacts to pain. The study of pain control has revealed that pain can be significantly reduced by a range of measures, including by assisting individuals to control their own treatment programmes and through altered mental states associated with meditation or concentration on activity. Yet, the limited availability of such measures to many people who could benefit extends this to the sphere of disability.

Social factors can, at the most fundamental level, define what is perceived as impairment. Perceptions of norms and differences vary culturally and historically. As mainstream perceptions change, people are defined in and out of impairment. Many people labelled 'mentally ill', for example, simply do not conform to contemporary social norms of behaviour. Other inequalities may contribute to the identification of impairment. For example, racist classifications in the school psychological service have led to a disproportionately high number of black compared to white children in segregated units for 'the emotionally and behaviourally disturbed', whilst it is relatively recently that the sexuality of lesbians and gay men has ceased to be officially defined as 'mental illness'.

Mainstream perceptions tend to increase the boundaries of impairment. The logical outcome of a successful disabled people's movement is a reduction in who is perceived as having an impairment. An absence of disability includes the widespread acceptance of individuality, through the development of a new norm which carries an expectation that there will be a wide range of attributes within a population. With an end to disability, many people currently defined as having an impairment will be within that norm. Impairment will only need definition as such if *in itself* it results in disadvantages such as pain, illness or reduced options.

Conclusion

I share the concerns expressed by some disabled people that some of the arguments I have put forward here could be used out of context to support the medical model of disability, to support the view that the experience of impairment is nothing but personal tragedy. However, suppression of our subjective experiences of impairment is not the answer to dealing with these risks; engaging with the debates and probing deeper for greater clarity might well be.

I am arguing for a recognition of the implications of impairment. I am not supporting traditional perspectives on disability and impairment, nor am I advocating any lessening of the energies we devote to eliminating disability. Acknowledging our personal experiences of impairment does not in any way disregard the tremendous weight of oppression, nor does it undermine our alignment with other civil rights movements. Certainly, it should not weaken our resolve for change. Disability remains our primary concern, *and* impairment exists alongside.

Integrating those key factors into our use of the social model is vital if we are to understand fully the ways that disability and impairment operate. What this renewed social model of disability does is broaden and strengthen the current social model, taking it beyond grand theory and into real life, because it allows us to incorporate a holistic understanding of our experiences and potential for change. This understanding needs to influence the structure of our movement – how we organise and campaign, how we include and support each other. A renewed approach to the social model is vital, both individually and collectively, if we are to develop truly effective strategies to manage our impairments and to confront disability. It is our learning and support within our own self-advocacy and political groups, peer counselling, training and arts that enable us to confront the difficulties we face, from both disability and impairment. It is this that allows us to continue working in the most effective way towards the basic principle of equality that underpins the disabled people's movement.

It is this confronting of disability and aspects of impairment that underpins the notion of disability pride which has become so central to our movement. Our pride comes not from 'being disabled' or 'having an impairment' but out of our response to that. We are proud of the way we have developed an understanding of the oppression we experience, of our work against discrimination and prejudice, of the way we live with our impairments.

A renewed approach to the social model is also relevant in our work with non-disabled people, particularly in disability equality training. Most of us who run such courses have avoided acknowledging impairment in our work, concerned that it confirms stereotypes of the 'tragedy' of impairment or makes the issues too complicated to convey. Denying the relevance of impairment, however, simply does not ring true to many non-disabled people: if pain, by definition, hurts then how can it be disregarded? We need to be honest about the experiences of impairment, without underplaying the overwhelming scale of disability. This does not mean portraying impairment as a total explanation, presenting participants with medical information or asking them to fantasise impairment through 'experiential' exercises. Instead, it allows a clear distinction to be made between disability and impairment, with an emphasis on tackling disabling barriers.

The assertion of the disabled people's movement that our civil and human rights must be protected and promoted by the removal of the disabling barriers of discrimination and prejudice has gained significant public support in recent years. It is this social model of disability which underpins the civil rights legislation for which we have campaigned, and civil rights will remain the centre of our political attention.

At a time when so many people – disabled and non-disabled – are meeting these ideas afresh, we need to be absolutely clear about the distinction between disability and impairment. The onus will remain upon disabled people to prove discrimination and there will still be attempts to refute our claims by using traditional perceptions of impairment. To strengthen our arguments we must peel away the layers and understand the complexities of the way disability and impairment work so that our allegations of discrimination are watertight. This is necessary now in our campaigning for full civil rights and will remain necessary when we claim justice under the legislation which will inevitably follow that campaign.

At this crossroads in disabled people's history, it is time for this renewed approach to the social model and the way we apply it. Disability is still socially created, still unacceptable, and still there to be changed; but by bringing impairment into our total understanding, by fully recognising our subjective experiences, we will achieve the best route to that change, the only route to a future which includes us all.

Notes

1 Along with many disabled people I feel some discomfort at the word impairment because it has become so imbued with offensive interpretation. Perhaps we need to replace impairment with an alternative term.

2 Professor Peter Singer, Director of the Centre for Human Bioethics, Monash University, Australia: quoted in Erika Feyerabend, 'Euthanasia in the Age of Genetic Engineering', *Reproductive and Genetic Engineering*, Vol. 2, No. 3, pp. 247–9, no date given.

3 For example, a medical law committee drawing up recommendations for withdrawing treatment from newborn babies with impairments, specifically excluded disabled adults or the parents of disabled children from the committee because 'the emotional discussion, which might have been likely, would have been very unhelpful and even counterproductive to the matter on hand', Prof Dr med. H.D. Hiersche in his introductory speech to the German Association of Medical Law on 'Limits on the Obligation to Treat Severely Handicapped Newborns', 27–29 June 1986.

4 A new screening test for Down's syndrome is recommended for all pregnant women on the grounds that the £88 test will reduce the cost per 'case' discovered (and, presumbly, aborted) from the current £43,000 to £29,500. See *Pulse*, 25 May 1991.

In an unpublished paper, a philosopher at Saarbrucken University in Germany used economic decision theory to quantify the value of life, including measuring which people should be subjected to involuntary euthanasia ('euthanasees'). Reported by Wilma Kobusch in a press statement; in *Gelenkirchen*, 5 November, 1991.

5 'Further Examples of Threats to Life', *Newsletter 13*; Disability Awareness in Action, January 1994.

References

Morris, Jenny (1994) 'Gender and Disability' in French, Sally, ed., *On Equal Terms: Working with disabled people*, Butterworth Heinemann.

Seale, Clive and Addington-Hall, Julia (1994) 'Euthanasia: why people want to die earlier' in *Social Science and Medicine*, Vol. 39, No. 5, pp. 647–54.

Union of the Physically Impaired Against Segregation (1976) *Fundamental Principles of Disability*, UPIAS.

United Nations Division for Economic and Social Information (1983) *World Programme of Action Concerning Disabled Persons*, United Nations.

NOTES ON THE CONTRIBUTORS

Nasa Begum is a research fellow at the Policy Studies Institute and was previously co-director of the Living Options Project at the King's Fund Centre. She is the author of *Burden of Gratitude: Women with disabilities receiving personal care* (1990) and *Something to be Proud Of . . . The Lives of Asian Disabled People and Carers in Waltham Forest* (1992).

Ruth Bailey is currently co-editor of *Disability Arts in London*. Her chapter in this book was originally written as a thesis for a Masters degree in social policy.

Liz Crow is a disabled feminist who has been active in the disabled people's movement for the past decade. Since 1987 she has worked as a disability equality consultant, particularly in the education, arts and media, and health sectors. Her published writing includes 'On our terms' in *Women's Art Magazine* (No. 47, July/August 1992); *Photography and Disability in England*, co-authored with Judith Crow and Andy Ormston, 1990); 'Disability in Children's Literature' in *Disability Arts in London* (February 1991); and *Disability Arts – The Business* (1994).

Sally French has always been visually impaired and went through special residential schools. She works half-time at Brunel University teaching psychology and sociology applied to health and illness, and disability studies. She also works freelance as a lecturer, researcher and writer. She is the editor of *On Equal Terms: working with disabled people* (1994) and *Disabling Barriers, Enabling Environments* (1993). She was on the course team for the Open University course 'The Disabling Society'.

Lois Keith works part-time teaching in an inner-city comprehensive and runs writing groups for adults. She has published books on English teaching and is the editor of *Mustn't Grumble: Writing by Disabled Women* (The Women's Press, 1994).

Margaret Kennedy has developed pioneering work in issues of disability and child protection. She is co-editor of *The ABCD Pack: Abuse and children who are disabled*. She chaired the Disability and Abuse Working Party of the British Association for the Study and Prevention of Child Abuse and Neglect and is a co-opted member of BASPCAN's national executive committee. She founded and chairs the Disability and Child Protection Forum. Margaret is disabled and a qualified nurse and social worker. She currently works as a freelance consultant and trainer on disability and child protection.

Julie McNamara says: 'I am a white, second generation Irish lesbian, working class and proud! I have been involved in the mental health system (on both sides of the fence) for 16 years now. During that time I worked as a Mental Health Co-ordinator in Hackney education service. I have been active in the disabled people's movement and Survivors Speak Out for some years now and am passionate about the campaign for 'Rights not Charity', piss on pity. At the time of writing this chapter I was interrupted by becoming the first Mental Health Co-ordinator to be taken on Section 136 of the Mental Health Act. I survived. And I will thrive . . .'

Jenny Morris is a freelance researcher and writer. She is currently researching the experiences of disabled children in the care system.

The Powerhouse is a group of disabled women (mainly women with learning difficulties) and non-disabled women who have successfully campaigned for a safe house for women with learning difficulties who have experienced abuse.

Ayesha Vernon has been working in the field of equal opportunities since 1990, first as a director of Peterborough Race Equality Council and then as a senior lecturer at Peterborough Regional College. She is currently completing her doctorate with the University of Leeds on the issue of simultaneous oppression and Black disabled women. She is a committed Black activist, feminist and disability activist. She works as a freelance consultant on race and disability matters. Publications include 'Why ethnic minority disabled people receive poorer quality services' in *Reflections: the views of Black disabled people on their lives and community care*, and 'Consumer choice and independent living for disabled people' in *The Future of Social Work*, a collection of seminar papers.

INDEX

Technologies of Truth

VISIBLE EVIDENCE

Edited by Michael Renov, Faye Ginsburg, and Jane Gaines

Public confidence in the "real" is everywhere in decline. This series offers a forum for the in-depth consideration of the representation of the real, with books that engage issues that bear upon questions of cultural and historical representation, and that forward the work of challenging prevailing notions of the "documentary tradition" and of nonfiction culture more generally.

VISIBLE EVIDENCE, VOLUME 2

Technologies of Truth

Cultural Citizenship and the Popular Media

Toby Miller

University of Minnesota Press

Minneapolis

London

Published by the University of Minnesota Press
111 Third Avenue South, Suite 290
Minneapolis, MN 55401-2520
http://www.upress.umn.edu

Series design by Will H. Powers
Typeset in Sabon and Memphis by Stanton Publication Services, Inc.

Library of Congress Cataloging-in-Publication Data

Miller, Toby.
    Technologies of truth : cultural citizenship and the popular media /
Toby Miller.
        p.   cm. — (Visible evidence ; 2)
    Includes bibliographical references and index.
    ISBN 0-8166-2984-6 (alk. paper). — ISBN 0-8166-2985-4 (alk. paper)
    1. Popular culture. 2. Mass media—Social aspects. 3. Arts and
society. 4. Masculinity in popular culture. 5. Culture conflict.
6. Politics and culture. 7. Prisoners in popular culture. I. Title. II. Series.
    HM101.M585   1998
    306—dc21   97-25952

Printed in the United States of America on acid-free paper

The University of Minnesota is an equal-opportunity educator and employer.

10 09 08 07 06 05 04 03 02 01 00 99 98   10 9 8 7 6 5 4 3 2 1